NURSERY CRAFTS

NURSERY CRAFTS

by

Jarie Lee Waterfall

HUMANICS LEARNING
The Most Trusted Name in Education

NURSERY CRAFTS

by
Jarie Lee Waterfall

HUMANICS LEARNING
The Most Trusted Name in Education
Humanics Learning is an imprint of Humanics Limited

HUMANICS LEARNING
P.O. Box 7447
Atlanta, Georgia 30309

Illustrations by Liza Gollobith

First Printing 1988

PRINTED IN THE UNITED STATES OF AMERICA

Library of Congress Cataloging-in-Publication Data

Waterfall, Jarie Lee
    Nursery Crafts.

1. Handicraft.   I. Title
TT157.W357   1988   745.5—dc19   CIP 87-25185
ISBN 0-89334-107-X

Dedicated to all the little children
who are very precious and very special to me

Table of Contents

Introduction

Nursery Crafts is a collection of projects and ideas for teachers of young children in pre-school and kindergarten. This collection will provide you with a variety of creative and fun activities.

Instructions and patterns have been provided for all activities so that the projects can be done easily and quickly.

The following suggestions may help you in using the activities in *Nursery Crafts:*

1. The instructions in this book are written so that you can adapt the activities to different age groups as needed. Small children may need extra help in cutting, gluing, marking, etc., while older children may be able to complete the activities independently.

2. Depending on the time available, you may want to have the pattern pieces, ribbon pieces, and other materials prepared and cut out ahead of time, and have the children assemble and decorate them.

3. Many of the activities suggest using mounting tape. This is a double-sided tape available at most hobby or hardware stores.

4. Ribbon, construction paper, and fabric are used in almost all of the activities. You may want to save small scraps of ribbon, construction paper, or fabric for future use.

5. When using marking pens, use water color markers. Permanent markers may bleed or run.

6. Use of a glue gun is suggested for many activities. This is an aid which will help you cut your project time in half and enable you to do projects that may otherwise be too time-consuming. The glue adheres quickly and dries almost instantly and is ideal for projects requiring drying time between steps. To use the glue gun, plug in and wait for it to warm up. Place a glue cartridge in the back and push. As the cartridge goes through the gun it melts and comes out the nose. Apply the glue. After it is applied, count to 20. The glue will still adhere at this point and will not be quite as hot.
   Caution: The glue gun is warm to the touch, but the glue inside is very hot. Children should not use it because there is a possibility of burns if not carefully handled and properly supervised.

7. Many of the projects in this book suggest the use of plastic moveable eyes. They bring the project to life, and children love the way they look and feel.
   However, care should be taken in using these eyes with small children. Since some children are likely to put things in their mouths, you may not want to use them with children under two years of age.

In order to minimize accidents, the use of plastic eyes has been limited to projects with very small creatures which require very small eyes. Please note, however, that you may always substitute small circles of black and white construction paper for the plastic eyes.

8. Included in this book are fingerplays, rhymes, and stories that relate to the projects. These are designed to be used after the project is completed and students have cleaned up.

Nursery Crafts was designed during a period of time in which I was directing a Nursery Program. All of the ideas and projects on the following pages were used with great delight.

Many of the leaders, teachers, and advisors who were familiar with my work asked many times to use my ideas and patterns. A need was clearly evident for a source of ideas for arts and crafts projects for use with small children. This was indeed a pleasure to write. Enjoy!

Objectives

Using the ideas in this book, learning can be enhanced by providing students with activities designed to foster growth in the following areas:

Fine motor skills—Every activity develops fine motor skills by providing practice in tracing, cutting, pasting, drawing, or coloring.

Social-emotional—Several activities are included to enhance the child's self-concept and self-awareness, and to promote self-help skills.

Cognitive—The fingerplays and stories included in the book help to develop the child's memory and imagination.

Language—All of the activities build skills in listening and following directions.

In addition, selected activities offer young children early experiences in the following curriculum areas:

Science—Activities are included to encourage awareness of plants, animals, insects, and nature.

Social Studies—Children learn about the different seasons of the year, and about different cultures.

Mathematics—Practice in matching, sequencing, and recognizing shapes helps promote early math skills.

Pre-reading—Many activities provide opportunities for practice in visual discrimination using shapes and colors.

The Role of Arts and Crafts

Art experiences play a vital role in the child's development, but do we really stop to think how much art affects the child's life?

Art builds perception. The child learns visual and tactile perception and artistic expression. Motor skills are developed—such as eye-hand coordination and large and small muscle development. We, as teachers, must not forget the basic purpose of art is to allow for self-expression. Other goals in our art program should include creativity, visual and tactile perception, and developing a feeling for art (aesthetic judgment). For children, art is not only a form of expressing one's feelings but also a way of communicating ideas.

The teacher plays a vital role in the child's artistic development and expression. She should understand the stages of development and help children express themselves creatively. She should have an understanding of human growth and development so she can anticipate, understand and cope with the behavior of the child.

The value of art activities for the young child lies primarily in the process of creation rather than in the finished product. This sense of accomplishment derived from successful manipulation of art media can help build self-confidence, a feeling of "I did this by myself. In enjoyed doing it. I'm pretty good." This is especially true if the child's creation is valued for itself and not compared to someone else's which might be more artistic or representative. Through experimentation and practice with some guidance, the child learns the possibilities, limits, and a beginning control of the media he uses. These learnings are important in themselves, and also as foundations for later learnings.

We must learn to respect children's art work. It has a distinct charm of its own. Children have a difficult time feigning the enjoyment of art, so we must be aware of a child who doesn't enjoy art and evaluate how we are presenting it. Remember that children are not concerned with using color imitatively as it appears in nature and they do not draw things the way they look to adults. Therefore, there is no place for stereotypes, mimeographed outlines, or coloring books. Every activity should be a creative experience which requires original thinking, planning, and doing. Children should be encouraged to create at their own speed and verbalize about what they are doing.

Remember that all children have the potential for creative expression. It is the responsibility of parents and teachers to provide opportunities for this potential to develop as fully as possible.

The Teacher of Art

New programs, classrooms and equipment are signs of progress, but the individual teacher is still the most vital factor in all our learning experiences. She should be the inspired one, creating and adapting new techniques, lighting the flame for greater achievement. This book tries to present practical suggestions within the basic principles of free expression for young children.

Creative art activities are based on the same precepts that apply to other forms of education. The teacher and group leaders have an even greater opportunity for devising new techniques in developing the creative instincts of students.

The following projects allow freedom and expression of self, therefore allowing much enjoyment for children. They require no special skill and will hold the interest of children.

Scissor Safety

Directions: Read each of the safety rules. (Teachers can read to small children.)

I cut only materials that I am supposed to cut.

I keep scissor points away from my face.

I take good care of my scissors.

If I must walk with scissors, I walk slowly with scissor points to the ground.

I hand scissors to other people by giving them the handle part.

I put my scissors in the proper storage place.

NURSERY CRAFTS

Airplane Pilot

Materials

- Glue
- Scissors
- One piece of colored posterboard for airplane
- One piece of white posterboard for propeller
- One brass brad fastener
- One straw
- One-½-inch pom-pom
- Small plastic moveable eyes

Instructions

1. Using pattern, cut airplane from colored posterboard.
2. Cut propeller from white posterboard.
3. Attach propeller to airplane using brass brad fastener. (You may want to first punch a hole with a paper punch.)
4. Cut straw to 2-½ inches and attach to inside of pom-pom with glue.
5. Attach eyes to pom-pom.
6. Glue straw with pom-pom to back of airplane.

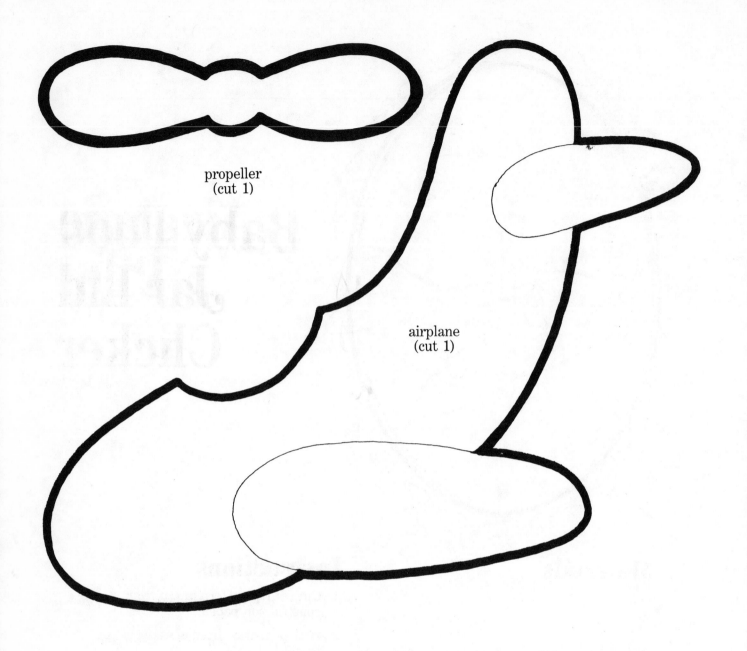

propeller
(cut 1)

airplane
(cut 1)

Children's Rhyme
Wings

Silver ships, high in the air:
Airplanes take us everywhere.
They leave their trails
Of white jet streams,
And transport us
In and out of dreams.

Baby Food Jar Lid Clicker

Materials

- Glue
- Scissors
- Marking pen
- Two plastic ¼-inch moving eyes
- One baby food jar lid
- One piece of brown construction paper for frog
- One piece of green construction paper for leaf
- One piece of white construction paper for lily

Instructions

1. Cut out the pattern pieces from construction paper.
2. With pen, draw front of water lily on pattern piece.
3. Glue the leaf onto the top of the jar lid, the water lily onto the leaf, and the frog onto the water lily. Glue eyes onto frog.
4. When the glue dries, press in the center of the jar lid, making a click-click noise.

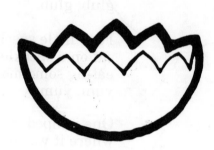

frog
(cut 1)

water lily
(cut 1)

leaf
(cut 1)

Five Little Speckled Frogs

Five little speckled frogs
sat on a speckled log
eating some most delicious bugs
yum, yum.

One jumped into the pool
where it was nice and cool
now there are four green speckled frogs
glub, glub.

Four little speckled frogs
sat on a speckled log
eating some most delicious bugs
yum, yum.

One jumped into the pool
where it was nice and cool
now there are three green speckled frogs
glub, glub.

Three little speckled frogs
sat on a speckled log
eating some most delicious bugs
yum, yum.

One jumped into the pool
where it was nice and cool
now there are two green speckled frogs
glub, glub.

Two little speckled frogs
sat on a speckled log
eating some most delicious bugs
yum, yum.

One jumped into the pool
where it was nice and cool
now there's just one green speckled frog
glub, glub.

One little speckled frog
sat on a speckled log
eating some most delicious bugs
yum, yum.

He jumped into the pool
where it was nice and cool
now there are no green speckled frogs
glub, glub.

Bee
and
Beehive

Materials

- Glue or glue gun
- Scissors
- Black marking pen
- One package of plastic straws for beehive
- One piece of poster board for base
- One piece of yellow sponge for bee
- Two plastic moving eyes, ¼-inch wide
- One piece of black construction paper for wings
- Sharpened pencil

Instructions

1. Cut out a small piece of poster board as the base for the beehive.

2. Cut straws in various lengths, from ¼ to 1 inch long. Glue straws to the base and each other in a standing position, one next to the other. Make sure one straw is taller than all the others, approximately 1¾-inch long.

3. Cut the bee out of the sponge, glue on wings and eyes. Draw stripes on body with marking pen.

4. With pencil, poke a shallow hole underneath sponge bee, fill with glue, and mount bee on tallest straw.

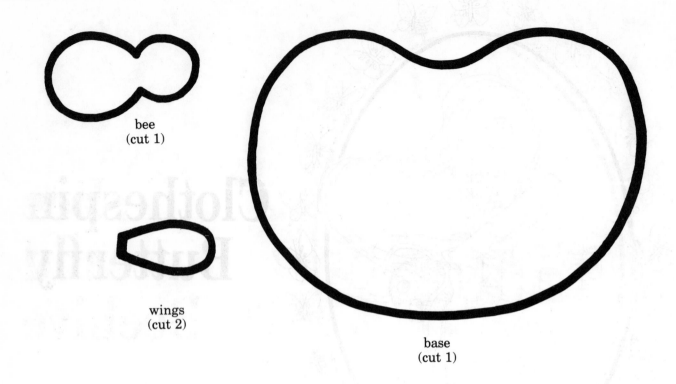

bee
(cut 1)

wings
(cut 2)

base
(cut 1)

Fingerplay
Beehive

Here is the beehive,
where is the bee?
Oh look; he's inside,
making honey for you and me!

Clothespin Butterfly

Materials

- Glue
- Scissors
- Clothespin for body
- Two plastic moving eyes, ¼-inch wide
- One 1-inch pom-pom for head
- Four pieces of brightly colored tissue paper for wings
- Two round colored stickers, ¾-inch wide, for decorating wings
- One pipe cleaner for antennae, 4½ inches long

Instructions

1. Cut out the wings from tissue paper, and layer them on top of each other.
2. Crinkle wings at center and fasten with clothespin. Separate tissue layers to make them look pretty.
3. Put stickers on wings.
4. Glue on pom-pom head and eyes.
5. Opening clothespin slightly, center pipe cleaner just behind pom-pom head and close clothespin.
6. Twist pipe cleaners together on top of clothespin and curl each end to look like antennae.

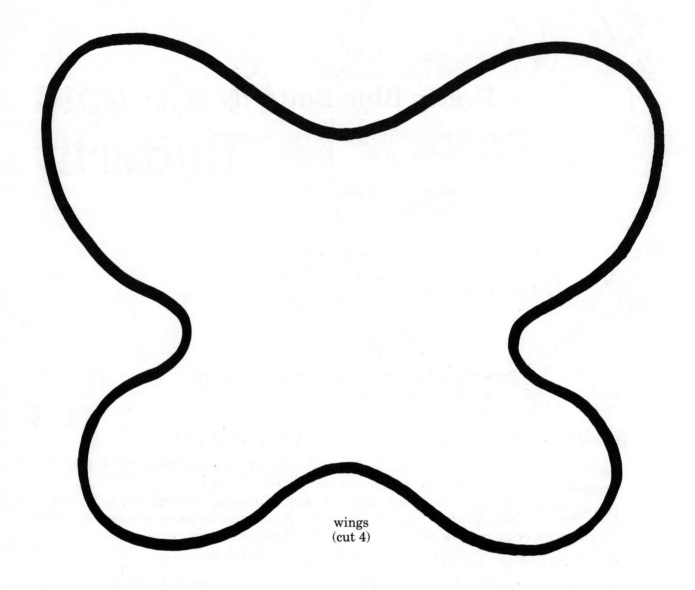

wings
(cut 4)

Children's Rhyme
Pretty Blue Butterfly

Pretty blue butterfly, spread your wings,
and glide, glide, glide.

Pretty blue butterfly, flap your wings,
fly higher and higher up into the sky.

Now butterfly blue, fold your wings tight
and fall and roll and drift to the earth,
and rest on a leaf for awhile, then dust
yourself off, and fly, fly, fly.

Fly my little butterfly, fly to the right,
fly to the left, and twirl, twirl, twirl.

Pretty blue butterfly, beautiful blue butterfly,
come, sit in the circle and rest.

Note: *If your class made butterflies in previous activities, they can use them in this one. Other fun things for this activity are scarfs, streamers, rags, crepe paper, nylons. If nothing is available, have the children spread their arms like wings. In this activity, children are to follow the leader and do what the verse says: glide, twirl, high, low, right, left, etc. Lots of fun!*

Cotton Ball Lamb

Materials

- Glue
- Scissors
- Eight to ten cotton balls
- Two plastic drinking straws
- One piece of scrap material
- One piece ¼-inch wide ribbon for bow
- Small plastic moveable eyes

Instructions

1. Glue cotton balls together to form lamb's body.

2. Use one cotton ball for lamb's head. Glue onto the lamb's body.

3. Cut plastic drinking straws into 3-inch lengths. Glue onto lamb's body.

4. Cut ears and tail from scrap material and glue onto lamb's body.

5. Glue eyes onto lamb's face.

6. Tie a small bow with ribbon and glue to top of lamb's head.

tail
(cut 1)

ears
(cut 2)

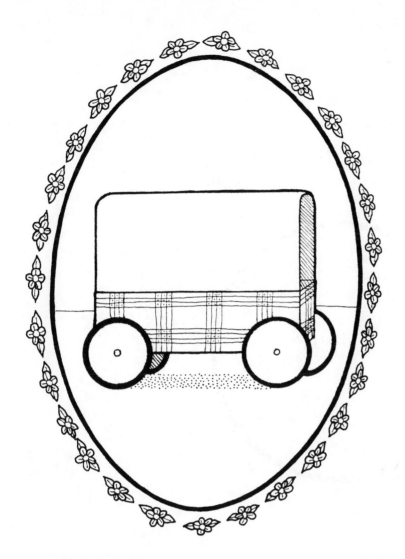

Covered Wagon

Materials

- Glue
- Scissors
- One small box
- One piece of brightly colored contact paper
- Four gold brad fasteners
- One piece of white construction paper
- Poster board for wheels

Instructions

1. Cover box with brightly colored contact paper. (If a small box is unavailable, you may also use poster board or construction paper to make a box.)

2. Cut out wheels from poster board. Using brad fasteners, attach wheels to wagon sides so that they turn.

3. Cut out wagon canvas from white construction paper and glue to the top of wagon, as illustrated. The *width* of the canvas should match the length of the wagon, and the *length* of the canvas should be 1½ times that. You may also staple or use a mounting tape.

4. Decorate the wagon if desired.

wheels
(cut 4)

Crazy Bird

Materials

- Glue
- Scissors
- Two plastic moving eyes, ¼-inch wide
- One small styrofoam egg (the size of a real egg)
- One 1½-inch pom-pom for head
- Four pipe cleaners for legs
- One package of feathers
- One 12-inch piece of ½-inch wide ribbon for bow

Instructions

1. Glue pom-pom head to large end of egg.
2. Glue on eyes and bow.
3. Place the pipe cleaner legs in the bottom of the egg at four different places (two in front, two in back). Curl the ends so that they will support the bird and it can stand by itself.
4. Push the feathers into the body so that they look like wings and a tail.

Dancing Valentine

Materials

- Glue
- Stapler
- Scissors
- Black marking pen
- One piece of red construction paper, for body, head, hands, and feet
- One package of ½-inch elastic
- Two yards red velvet ribbon (or red and white polka dot), ¼ inch wide
- Black/white construction paper for eyes

Instructions

1. Cut out pattern pieces for valentine head and body. Staple head to the body, overlapping the points.

2. Cut elastic into four 5½-inch lengths for arms and legs. Staple the pieces to the back of the body at the marked points.

3. Cut 2 hands and 2 feet and staple to the ends of the elastic.

4. To make the handle, cut ribbon to a 10-inch length, fold in half, and staple to the top of the head.

5. Cut tiny red heart and glue on or staple to the body.

6. Tie ribbon into four small bows and glue on or staple in place.

7. Glue on the eyes. Use marking pen to make nose and mouth.

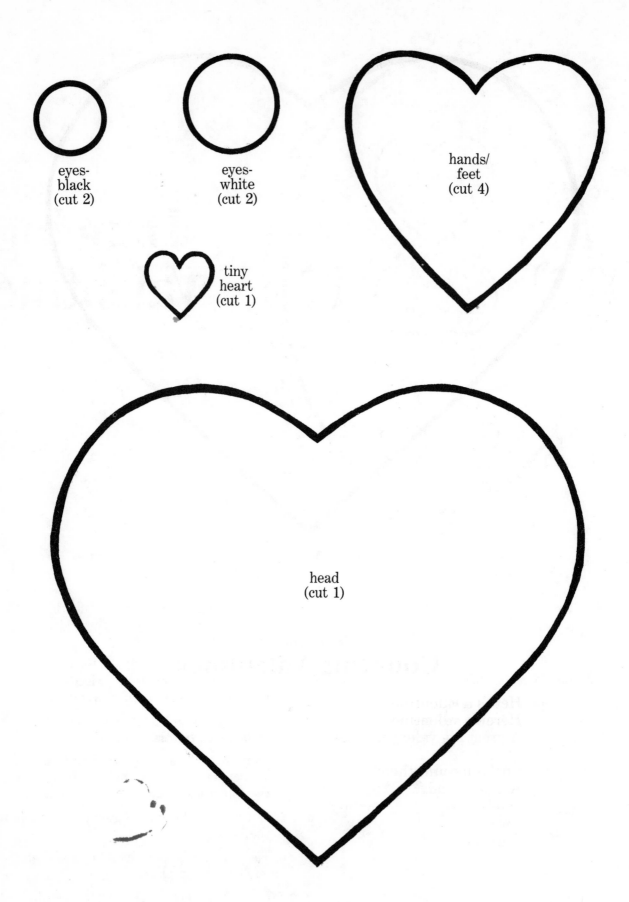

eyes-
black
(cut 2)

eyes-
white
(cut 2)

hands/
feet
(cut 4)

tiny
heart
(cut 1)

head
(cut 1)

body
(cut 1)

Counting Valentines

Here's a valentine.
Here's a valentine.
A great big valentine I see. *(hands over head, pointed down)*

Can you count them?
Are you ready?
One!
Two!
Three!

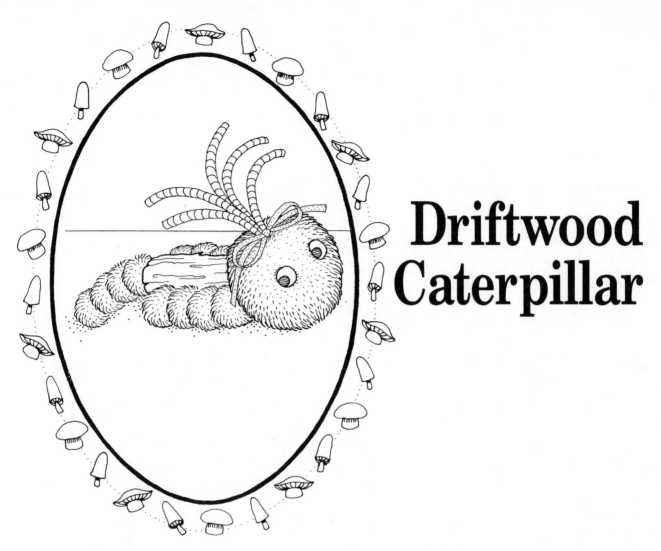

Driftwood Caterpillar

Materials

- Glue or glue gun
- One small piece of driftwood (about 3 inches long) for body
- One 1½-inch yellow pom-pom for head
- Twelve ½-inch yellow pom-poms for legs and tail
- Two plastic ¼-inch moving eyes
- One ribbon, ⅛-inch wide, 6 inches long
- Five strands of yarn, each 2 inches long, for hair

Instructions

1. Glue head and legs on driftwood. Glue remaining pom-poms together for a tail, and glue onto driftwood.

2. Glue on eyes.

3. Lay ribbon on flat surface, and place yarn on top of ribbon. Tie ribbon and make a bow. Trim yarn so that it sticks out of ribbon on one side (for hair), and is cut close to ribbon on other side.

4. Glue ribbon with yarn to top of head, so that hair sticks straight up.

Driftwood Friend

Materials

- Glue or glue gun
- Scissors
- Black marking pen
- Black/white construction paper for eyes
- One piece of driftwood (approximately 6 inches long, ³/₁₄-inch around), flat at one end, for body
- One 2-inch styrofoam ball for head
- One ½-inch pom-pom for nose
- One piece of brown poster board for shoes
- One piece of scrap material or ribbon for arms

Instructions

1. Cut out pattern pieces.
2. Glue the flat end of driftwood to shoes.
3. Glue arms on.
4. Push styrofoam ball onto driftwood.
5. Using a little glue, glue on eyes, hair, and nose.
6. Draw mouth and shoelaces with marking pen.

eyes-
black
(cut 2)

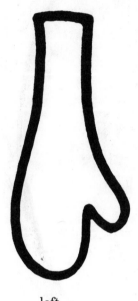

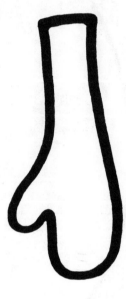

eyes-
white
(cut 2)

left
arm
(cut 1)

right
arm
(cut 1)

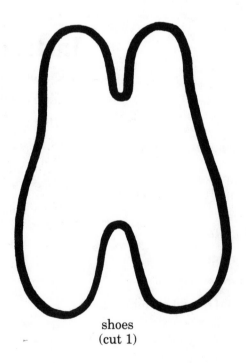

shoes
(cut 1)

Easter Rabbit

Materials

- Glue
- Scissors
- Marking pen
- Knife
- Two ¼-inch moving eyes
- One styrofoam egg, 3 inches long, 2 inches wide
- Three very small straw flowers
- One 6 × 7-inch piece of white construction paper for rabbit
- One piece of pink construction paper for tummy and inside ears
- One 4 × 3-inch piece of poster board (any color) for base
- One 6-inch long, ¼-inch wide ribbon

Instructions

1. Cut out patterns.
2. Using marking pen, draw nose, whiskers, and mouth, and outline the legs.
3. Glue on eyes, tummy, and inside of ears.
4. Cut stems off of dried flowers and glue onto rabbit's forehead.
5. Tie bow and glue it onto rabbit.
6. Cut a tiny slice off large end of egg. Glue cut end of egg to base.
7. Fold side flaps on bunny around styrofoam egg, insert one flap into the other, and glue in place.

tummy
(cut 1)

inside
of ears
(cut 2)

body
(cut 1)

Mrs. Easter Chicken

Storyteller: Do you know where the Easter Bunny gets Easter eggs? Well, of course, bunnies don't lay eggs. Chickens do. There is a special chicken who lays Easter eggs for the Easter bunny. Her name is Mrs. Easter Chicken. Mrs. Easter Chicken lives on a farm in a chicken house with all the other chickens. The other chickens sit on their nests and lay plain white eggs, the kind you eat for breakfast. But Mrs. Easter Chicken has a magic nest. When she sits on her magic nest, she lays Easter eggs . . . red and yellow and pink and blue Easter eggs.

Now, Mrs. Easter Chicken has a real problem. She loves to eat. One year right before Easter, Mrs. Easter Chicken ate too many goodies. She ate candy bars, angel food cake, chocolate ice cream, strawberry shortcake, lemon pie, banana pudding, blueberry muffins, waffles with maple syrup, a hot fudge sundae, a vanilla milkshake and pancakes with ice cream and butterscotch sauce! But the worst was yet to come!

The day before Easter, she got on her magic nest to lay Easter eggs, just like she always did. She laid beautiful Easter eggs . . . red and yellow and pink and blue eggs. Lots of Easter eggs. But!! When Mrs. Easter Chicken tried to get off her magic nest, she was stuck. She was so fat from all the goodies she'd eaten that she couldn't get off her magic nest. Mrs. Easter Chicken said:

Mrs. Easter Chicken: "Well, I do declare, I seem to be stuck to my magic nest."

Storyteller: The other chickens shook their heads, flapped their aprons and clucked:

Other Chickens: "My, my. Poor Mrs. Easter Chicken."

Storyteller: Early Easter morning Mr. Easter Bunny came hippity-hopping to the chicken house to fill up his basket with Easter eggs.

Easter Bunny: "Get up please, Mrs. Easter Chicken. I need my Easter eggs."

Storyteller: Mrs. Easter Chicken said:

Mrs. Easter Chicken: "I do declare, Mr. Easter Bunny, I seem to be stuck to my magic nest. I can't get up."

Storyteller: The other chickens shook their heads, flapped their aprons and said:

Other Chickens: "My, my. Poor Mrs. Easter Chicken."

Storyteller: Mr. Easter Bunny said:

Easter Bunny: "Oh, dear! What will I do?"

Storyteller: The dog heard all the commotion and came to see what was going on. Mr. Easter Bunny said:

Easter Bunny: "I beg your pardon, Mr. Dog, but we need some help. Mrs. Easter Chicken is stuck to her magic nest. How can I get her up?"

Mr. Dog: "Put your arms around her and pull hard."

Storyteller: Mr. Easter Bunny put his arms around her and pulled as hard as he could, but still Mrs. Easter Chicken was stuck to her magic nest. The chickens shook their heads, flapped their aprons and clucked:

Other Chickens: "My, My. Poor Mrs. Easter Chicken."

Storyteller: The cat heard all the commotion and came to see what was going on. Mr. Easter Bunny said:

Easter Bunny: "I beg your pardon, Mr. Cat, but we need some help. Mrs. Easter Chicken is stuck to her magic nest. How can I get her up?"

Mr. Cat: "Put your arms around her and shake her."

Storyteller: Mr. Easter Bunny put his arms around Mrs. Easter Chicken and shook her as hard as he could, but Mrs. Easter Chicken was still stuck to her magic nest. The other chickens shook their heads, flapped their aprons and said:

Other Chickens: "My, my. Poor Mrs. Easter Chicken."

Storyteller: The pig heard all the commotion and came to see what was going on. Mr. Easter Bunny said:

Easter Bunny: "I beg your pardon, Mr. Pig, but we need some help. Mrs. Easter Chicken is stuck to her magic nest. How can I get her up?"

Mr. Pig: "Turn the magic nest upside down and she will fall out."

Storyteller: Mr. Easter Bunny turned the magic nest upside down, but Mrs. Easter Chicken was still stuck to her magic nest. The other chickens shook their heads, flapped their aprons and clucked:

Other Chickens: "My, my. Poor Mrs. Easter Chicken."

Storyteller: Well, all the commotion in the chicken house had stirred up the dust. Mrs. Easter Chicken's nose began to tickle. It tickled and tickled. All at once Mrs. Easter Chicken sneezed.

Mrs. Easter Chicken: "Kerr-chooo!"

Storyteller: Up she came! The other chickens flapped their aprons and said:

Other Chickens: "Thank goodness Mrs. Easter Chicken came unstuck!"

Storyteller: Mr. Easter Bunny filled his basket with the red and yellow and pink and blue Easter eggs. He said:

Easter Bunny: "Thank you very much Mrs. Easter Chicken."

Storyteller: He hippity-hopped away to hide the Easter eggs for the children. Mrs. Easter Chicken said:

Mrs. Easter Chicken: "Well, I do declare! I guess I'll have to go on a diet."

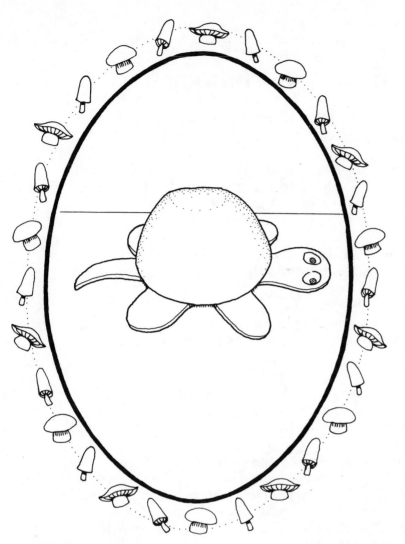

Egg Carton Turtle

Materials

- Glue
- Scissors
- One egg cup from an egg carton, cut and trimmed
- One piece of green felt for turtle's body
- Two plastic moving eyes, ¼-inch or smaller

Instructions

1. Glue egg cup onto the green felt body.
2. Glue on the eyes.
3. After children have cleaned up, read the story *Licorice the Pioneer* on the next page.

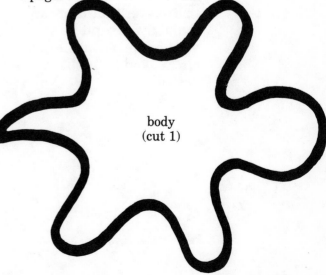

body
(cut 1)

Licorice the Pioneer

I want to tell you a story about a very special turtle named Licorice and his friend Josh.

Josh was a boy about five years old, and he was the best friend of our special turtle Licorice. Josh and Licorice were pioneers and they were getting ready to travel in a covered wagon across the plains many, many miles from their home.

I'll bet you all know why Josh named his turtle Licorice. That's right, it's because the turtle loved to nibble and eat licorice sticks.

When it was time to leave and travel in the covered wagon, Josh made sure that he had plenty of licorice sticks for his turtle to eat.

Licorice and Josh were brave pioneers and sometimes Licorice rode in Josh's pocket while they were traveling. Licorice didn't mind the hot weather but he did shiver in the cold.

Licorice got lost once. Josh was very upset and he called and called for Licorice. "Everyone help me call for Licorice!" *(Note to Teacher: Have the children participate and call for Licorice.)* Josh finally found Licorice and do you know where he was? He was in a drawer fast asleep. The wagons had gotten so heavy that they couldn't make it up the hills. The pioneers had to take some of their furniture out and leave it behind, and Licorice was asleep in a chest of drawers. Josh was so glad when he found his friend.

Licorice and Josh made it across the plains safely and made a new home for themselves.

Licorice lived to be a very old turtle and it didn't take him long to discover that there were other turtles there, too. Licorice found a wife and he settled down, had a lot of children, and lived very happily. But Licorice never outgrew his love for licorice sticks, and he nibbled on licorice every time he saw his friend Josh.

Flower Cut-Outs

Materials

- Glue
- Scissors
- One large piece of light blue construction paper for background
- One piece of red construction paper for petals
- One piece of green construction paper for stem and leaf
- One 1½-inch yellow pom-pom for flower center

Instructions

1. Cut out flower pieces and glue onto background.
2. Glue the pom-pom in the center of the flower.

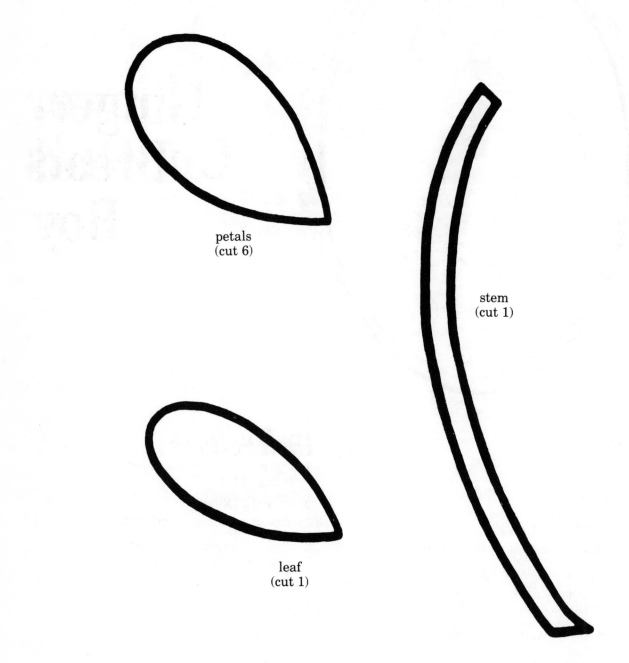

petals
(cut 6)

leaf
(cut 1)

stem
(cut 1)

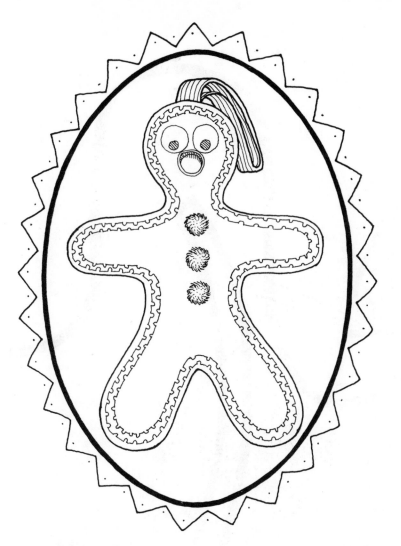

Ginger-Bread Boy

Materials

- Stapler
- Glue
- Scissors
- Black/white construction paper for eyes
- One large brown piece of construction paper for body
- One bottle cap for nose
- Three ½-inch pom-poms for buttons
- One piece of ribbon, 9-inches long and 1-inch wide, folded in half for handle
- One piece of gold braid or rickrack (optional), 48-inches long

Instructions

1. Cut out patterns.
2. Staple handle to top of head.
3. Glue on eyes, nose, and buttons.
4. Glue on rickrack around edges of gingerbread boy.

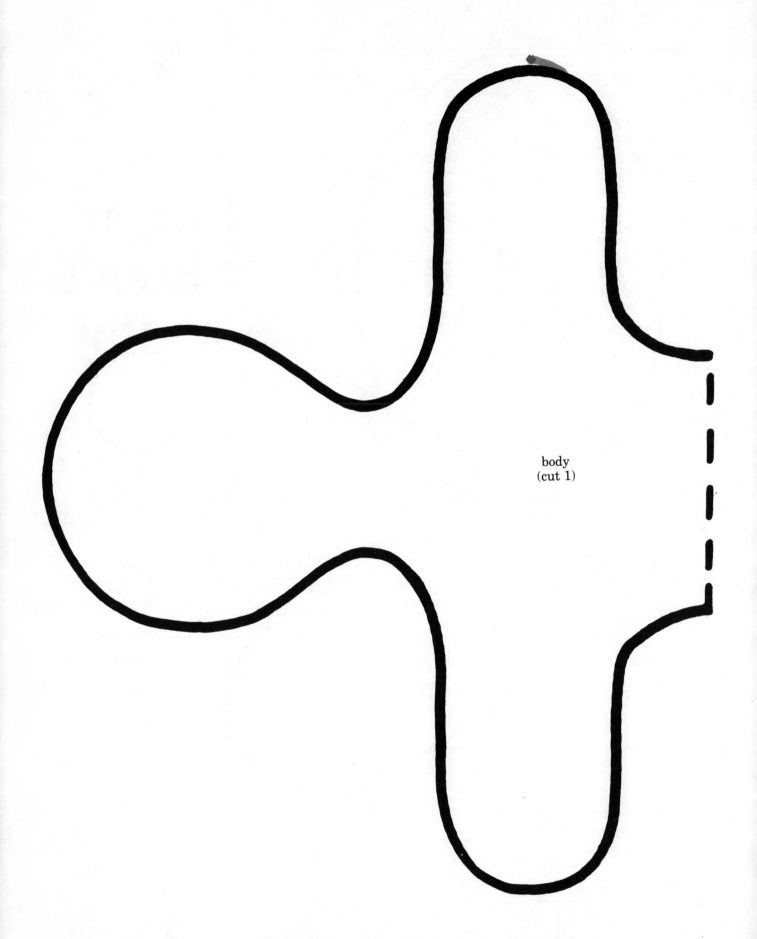

body
(cut 1)

Nursery Crafts

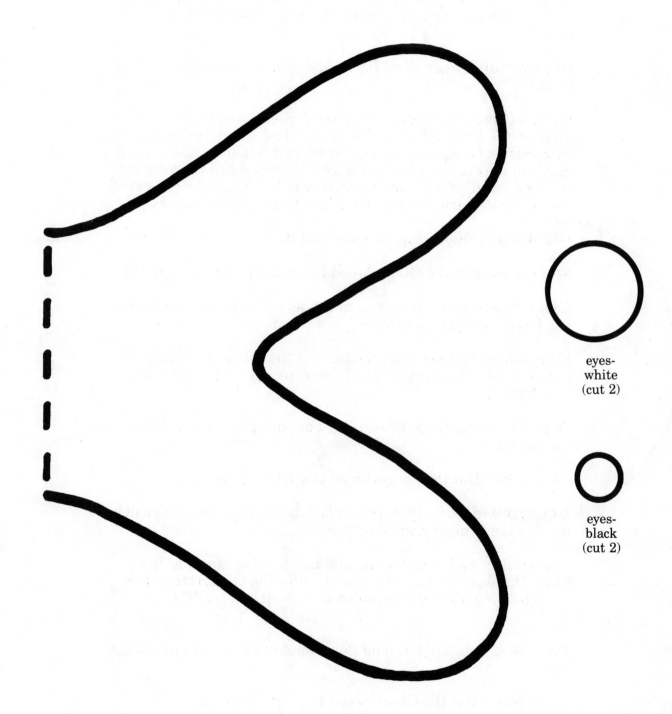

eyes-
white
(cut 2)

eyes-
black
(cut 2)

The Gingerbread Boy

Storyteller: Once upon a time there was a little old woman and a little old man who had no children. The Little Old Woman said:

Old Woman: "Sakes alive! It's lonely around here with no children."

Storyteller: So she decided to make a gingerbread boy to surprise the little old man. She made a fine Gingerbread Boy with raisins for his eyes and a cherry for his mouth. She popped him into the oven to bake. After awhile she opened the oven to see if he was finished. That Gingerbread Boy jumped right out of the oven and started to run away. The Little Old Woman said:

Old Woman: "Stop, stop, Gingerbread Boy."

Storyteller: But the Gingerbread Boy ran out the door saying:

Gingerbread Boy: "Run, run as fast as you can. You can't catch me. I'm the Gingerbread Man."

Storyteller: And ran away he did! But the Little Old Woman ran after him. The Gingerbread Boy ran on until he met a dog. The dog said:

Dog: "Stop, stop, Gingerbread Boy I am hungry and I want to eat you up."

Storyteller: But the Gingerbread Boy ran on, saying:

Gingerbread Boy: "Run, run as fast as you can. You can't catch me. I'm the Gingerbread Man."

Storyteller: And run away he did! But the dog ran after the Little Old Woman who was running after the Gingerbread Boy.
The Gingerbread Boy ran on until he met a cat. The cat said:

Cat: "Stop, stop, Gingerbread Boy. I am hungry and I want to eat you up."

Storyteller: But the Gingerbread Boy ran on saying:

Gingerbread Boy: "Run, run as fast as you can. You can't catch me. I'm the Gingerbread Man."

Storyteller: And run away he did! But the cat ran after the dog who was running after the Little Old Woman who was running after the Gingerbread Boy.

The Gingerbread Boy ran on until he met a pig. The pig said:

Pig: "Stop, stop, Gingerbread Boy. I am hungry and I want to eat you up."

Storyteller: But the Gingerbread Boy ran on saying:

Gingerbread Boy: "Run, run as fast as you can. You can't catch me. I'm the Gingerbread Man."

Storyteller: And run away he did! But the pig ran after the cat who was running after the dog who was running after the Little Old Woman who was running after the Gingerbread Boy.

The Gingerbread Boy ran on until he met a fox by the river. The Fox said:

Fox: "Here, Gingerbread Boy, jump on my back and I will carry you across the river so the pig, the cat, the dog, and the Little Old Woman won't catch you."

Gourd Indian

Materials

- Glue
- Scissors
- Straight Pins
- One small gourd
- One 2-inch styrofoam ball for head
- One ½-inch pom-pom for nose
- Black/white construction paper for eyes
- One feather
- One piece of colored construction paper for headband, feet, and hands

Instructions

1. Push the styrofoam ball head down on the small end of the gourd, making a small indentation.
2. Place a small amount of glue in the indentation and attach the head to the body.
3. Cut 2 feet and 2 hands from construction paper.
4. Glue the feet to the bottom of the body (large end of gourd). Secure with a straight pin until dry.
5. Glue the arms onto body. Secure with a straight pin until dry.
6. Glue eyes and nose on face.
7. Glue headband and feather on head.

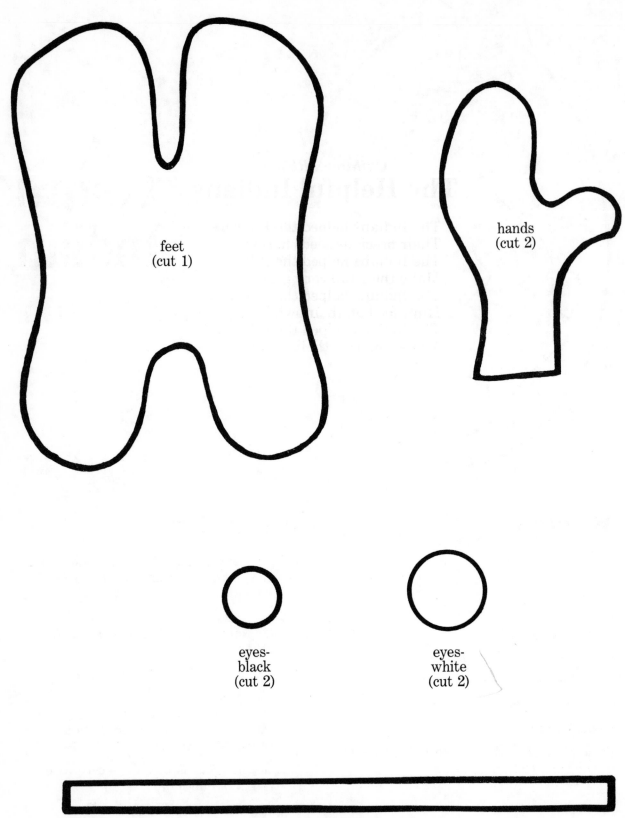

feet
(cut 1)

hands
(cut 2)

eyes-
black
(cut 2)

eyes-
white
(cut 2)

headband
(cut 1)

Children's Rhyme

The Helpful Indians

The Indians helped the Pilgrims
Their precious seeds to sow.
The Indians helped the Pilgrims
Make their tall corn grow.
The Indians helped the Pilgrims
Hunt food on their own.
The Indians helped the Pilgrims
Make America their home.

Hands on Stick

Materials

- Scissors
- Glue or glue gun
- Fine black marking pen
- One piece of white posterboard
- Ribbon for bow
- One ¼-inch dowel, 7 inches long
- Watercolors
- Brush
- Water

Instructions

1. Trace the child's hand on heavy paper.
2. Have the child paint the hand with water-colors, using a pale light color.
3. Cut out the hand.
4. Glue the hand to the dowel.
5. Tie a bow with the ribbon and glue onto hand.
6. Have the child write or print his name and the year. (You may have to write it for the child or provide help.)

Fingerplay
This Is My Hand

This is my hand,
This is my hand,
1, 2, 3, 4, 5.

This is my hand,
This is my hand,
Wave up high to the sky.

This is my hand,
This is my hand,
Clap, clap, clap, and click, click, click.

This is my hand,
This is my hand,
1, 2, 3, 4, 5.

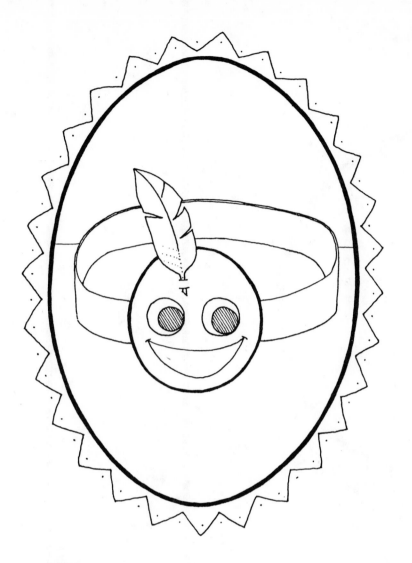

Head Band

Materials

- Glue
- Stapler
- Black marking pen
- One piece of colored construction paper for head band
- One piece of yellow construction paper for face
- One feather
- Black/white construction paper for eyes

Instructions

1. Using pattern, cut 3 head band pieces and staple together, overlapping ends, to form one long band.

2. Measure band to child's head and staple final seam together to fit.

3. Cut out face from yellow construction paper.

4. Cut an insert for feather in face. Place feather in insert, using a small amount of glue to adhere.

5. Glue on eyes and draw a mouth. (You may want to write child's name in where the mouth is drawn.)

6. Staple the face to the band.

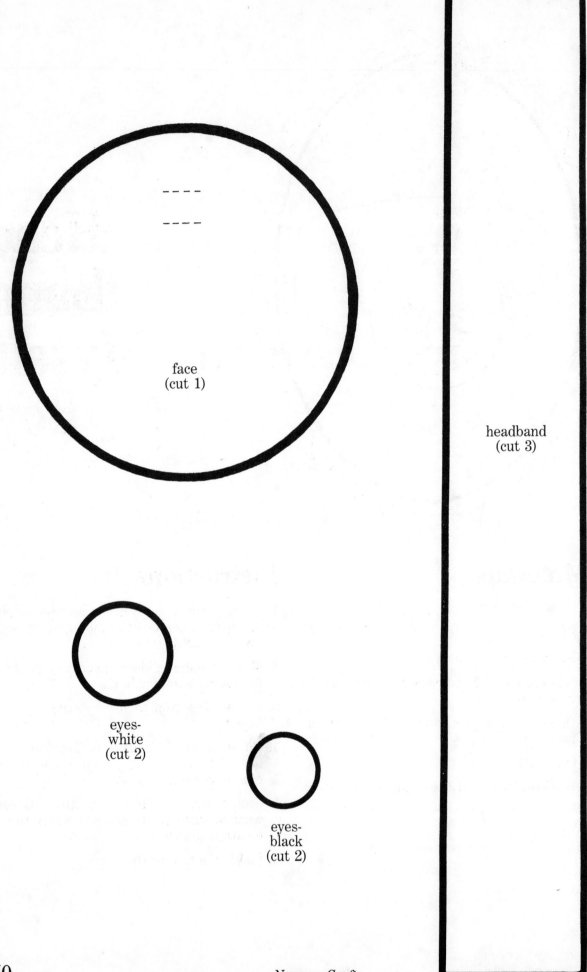

face
(cut 1)

eyes-
white
(cut 2)

eyes-
black
(cut 2)

headband
(cut 3)

I Can Dress Myself Boy

Materials

- Glue or glue gun
- Scissors
- Marking pen
- One piece of white poster board for body and arms
- Watercolors
- Paint brush
- Two plastic moving eyes, ¼-inch wide
- Four buttons
- One piece of string about 12 inches long (for lacing)
- Heavy piece of scrap fabric for outfit
- One adhesive backed piece of velcro
- Two brad fasteners

Instructions

1. Cut out patterns. Draw detail on boy using marking pen.

2. Color the doll with watercolors.

3. Fasten arms to doll with brad fasteners.

4. Glue on eyes.

5. Glue buttons to front of outfit. Let dry.

6. Lace around buttons with string and tie a bow.

7. Attach velcro to front of doll and back of outfit.

8. Attach outfit to body by bringing velcro together.

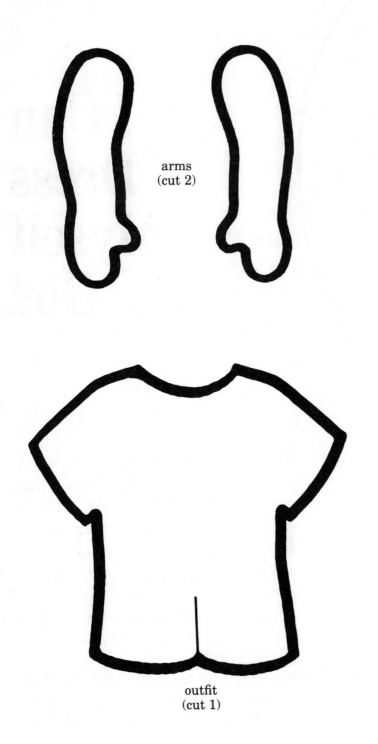

arms
(cut 2)

outfit
(cut 1)

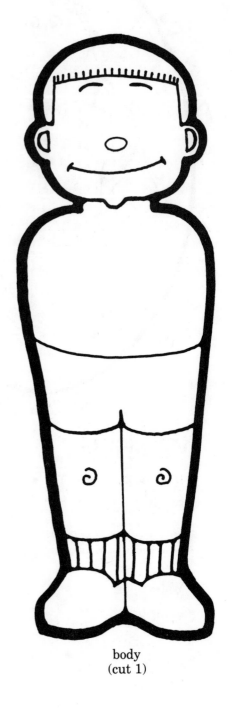

body
(cut 1)

I Can Dress Myself Girl

Materials

- Glue or glue gun
- Scissors
- Marking pen
- One piece of white poster board for body and arms
- Watercolors
- Paint brush
- Two plastic moving eyes, ¼-inch wide
- Three buttons
- One piece of string about 12 inches long (for lacing)
- Two pieces of ribbon, ⅛-inch wide, for hair bows
- Heavy piece of scrap fabric for dress
- One adhesive backed piece of velcro
- Two brad fasteners
- One piece of lace, 2½ × ½ inches

Instructions

1. Cut out patterns. Draw detail on girl using marking pen.
2. Color the doll with watercolors.
3. Fasten arms to doll with brad fastener.
4. Glue on eyes.
5. Make bows from ribbon and glue them on hair.
6. Glue lace and buttons on dress. Let dry.
7. Lace around buttons with string and tie a bow.
8. Attach velcro to front of doll and back of dress.
9. Attach outfit to body by bringing velcro together.

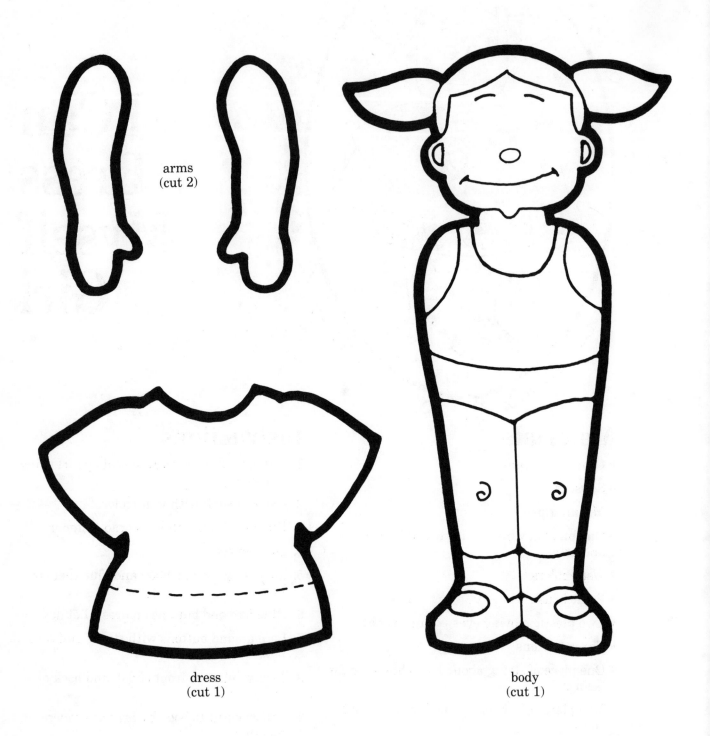

arms
(cut 2)

dress
(cut 1)

body
(cut 1)

Nursery Crafts

Children's Rhyme
All By Myself

I can get dressed all by myself,
And I think that I look neat.
But Mommy always says to me,
"Your shoes're on the wrong feet!"

How can they be the wrong feet?
They both belong to me.
They are the only feet I have,
And they sure look *right* to me!

I Can Share

Materials

- Glue
- Scissors
- Black marking pen
- One piece of yellow construction paper for card
- One 16-inch piece of rick-rack
- One small piece of flesh-colored felt for face
- One small piece of green felt for ball
- One small piece of red felt for storybook
- One small piece of orange felt for train
- Black/white construction paper for eyes
- One piece of ribbon, 7 inches long, ¼ inch wide, for bow

Instructions

1. Fold yellow construction paper in half, like a book.

2. Cut out a heart shape on the front of the card.

3. Cut the rick-rack into two 8-inch lengths. Glue around edges of the heart on front of card.

4. Using black marking pen, draw the person on the inside of the card, so that the face will show through the cut-out heart. Print "I Can Share" above the person.

5. Cut out the flesh-colored felt face and glue in place. Glue bow to top of head.

6. Cut eyes from construction paper and glue onto face.

7. Draw a smile and a nose on the face, using black marking pen.

8. Cut out the toys from scrap felt and glue them to inside of card.

9. Draw lines on the ball, a window on the train, and the word "Storybook" on the book, using the black marking pen.

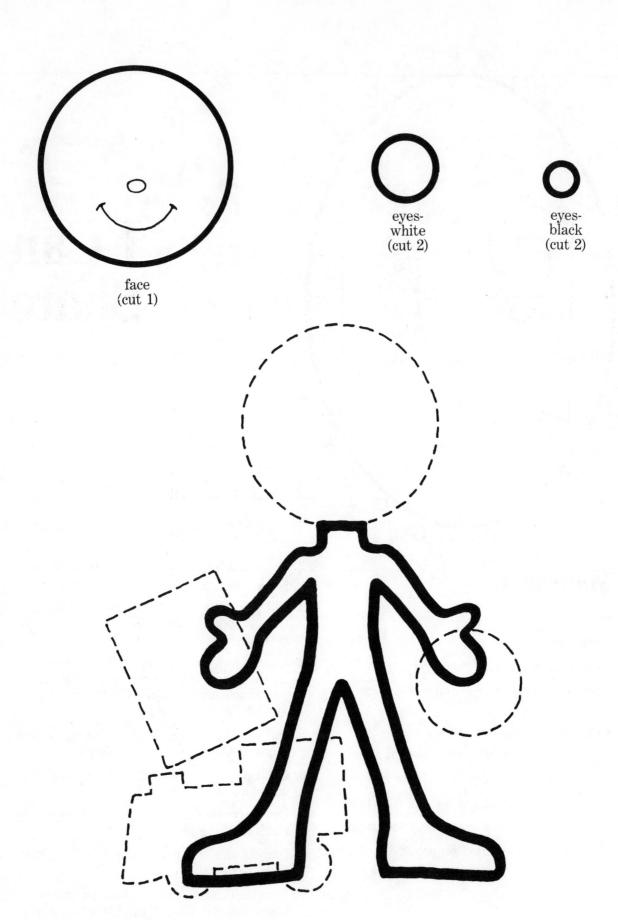

face
(cut 1)

eyes-
white
(cut 2)

eyes-
black
(cut 2)

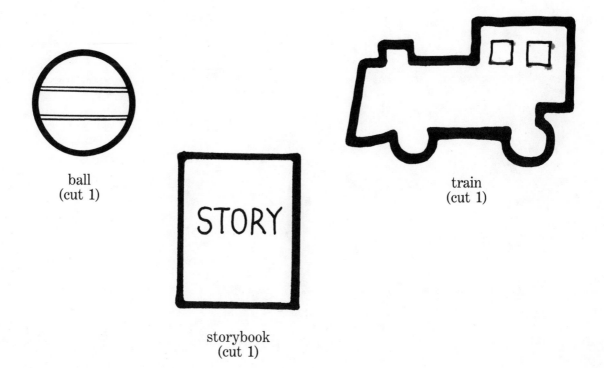

ball
(cut 1)

STORY

storybook
(cut 1)

train
(cut 1)

heart
pattern

Kite

Materials

- Glue or stapler
- Scissors
- Black/white construction paper for eyes
- One large piece of colored construction paper for kite body
- One 4-inch long, ½-inch wide ribbon for handle
- One 6-inch long, ¼-inch wide ribbon for bow
- Three small scrap ribbons for tail ties
- One 15-inch long piece of string
- One small piece of red felt for mouth

Instructions

1. Cut out patterns provided.
2. Fold handle ribbon in half and glue or staple to the back of kite.
3. Glue or staple on the bow.
4. Glue on the eyes and mouth.
5. Cut two small inserts for the string and then glue or staple it on.
6. Tie the tail ties onto the string.

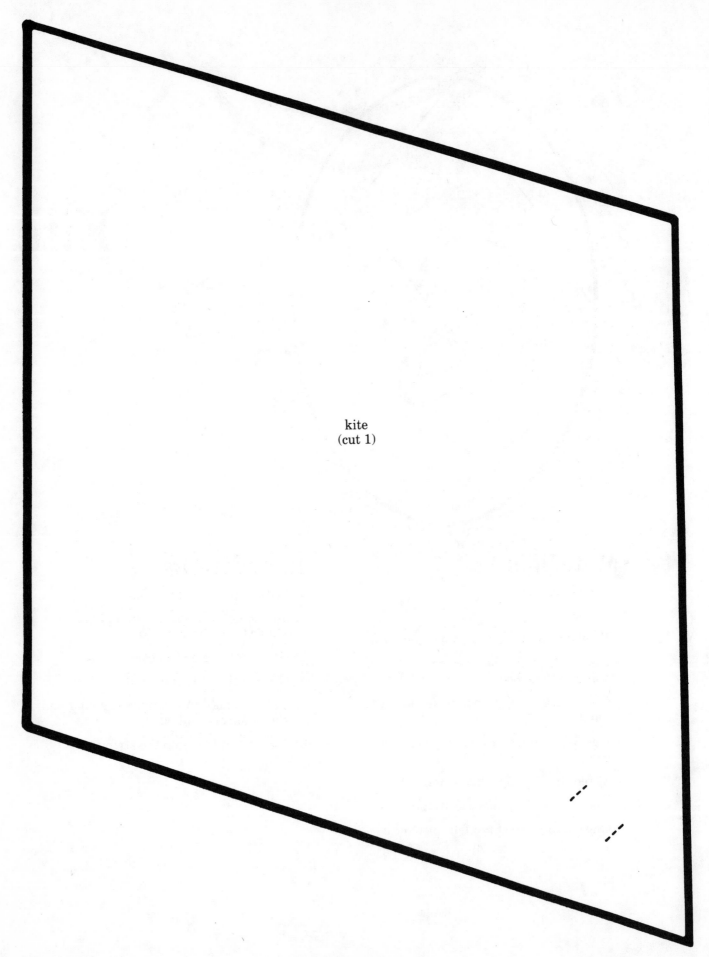

kite
(cut 1)

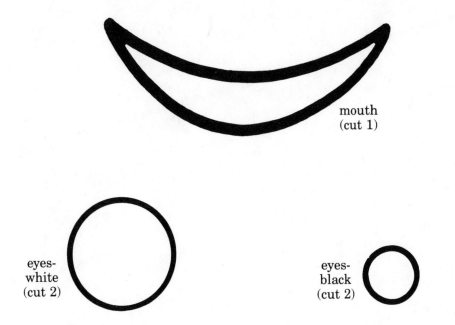

mouth
(cut 1)

eyes-
white
(cut 2)

eyes-
black
(cut 2)

Fingerplay
Kites

Five bright kites I bought at the store. *(hold up five fingers)*
Along came a strong wind, and now I have four. *(thumb down)*
Four bright kites flying over the sea.
Along came a big wave, and now I have three. *(index down)*
Three bright kites, I'll give one to you.
Three bright kites, now I have two. *(middle down)*
Two bright kites flew too near to the sun.
Poor little kites! Now I have one. *(ring down)*
One bright kite—that's enough for me,
I'll keep it away from the kite-eating tree!

Love's Baby

Materials

- Glue
- Scissors
- Stapler
- Black/white construction paper for eyes
- One piece of pink construction paper for baby
- One piece of white construction paper for diaper
- One piece of blue construction paper, 9 inches long, 6 inches wide, for blanket
- One 2-inch round mirror

Instructions

1. Cut out patterns and glue eyes and diaper on baby.

2. Make blanket by folding the blue construction paper in half and stapling the sides, leaving the top open like an envelope.

3. Glue the mirror onto the front.

4. Slip baby into blanket.

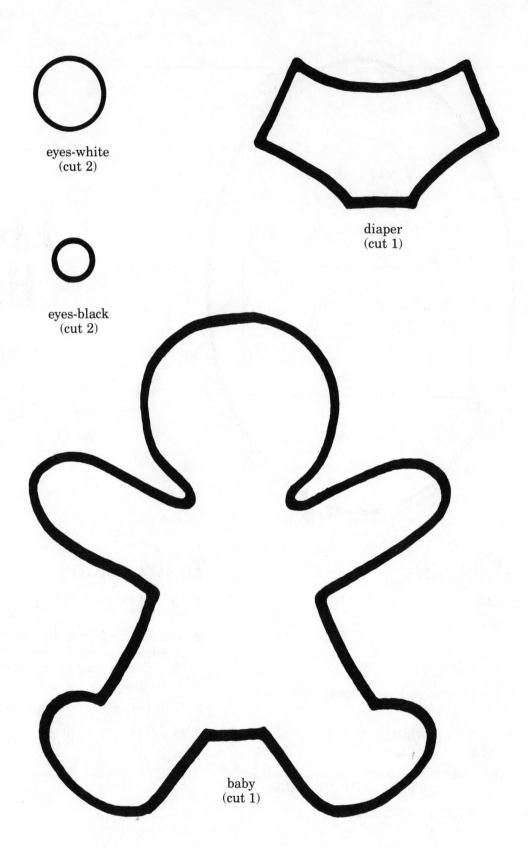

eyes-white
(cut 2)

diaper
(cut 1)

eyes-black
(cut 2)

baby
(cut 1)

Merry Christmas Snow Scene

Materials

- Glue
- One baby food bottle with lid
- One small plastic scene (a house, tree, or small manager scene)
- One package of white sequins (flower type)
- One package of small white plastic sequins
- One piece of ribbon, 10 inches long and ½ inch wide
- One 7-inch piece of gold braid
- One small piece of mounting tape

Instructions

1. The day before this project, glue the plastic scene to the inside of the lid of the jar. Allow to dry.

2. Turn the jar upright. Fill jar with 8-10 flower-type sequins and one tablespoon of small plastic sequins. (Children enjoy this and can handle it alone.)

3. Fill each jar with water, leaving a small space at top of jar. Make sure that the edge around the jar is dry so that the glue will set.

4. Apply glue all around the jar lid and place lid on jar. Make sure that the seal is tight.

5. Glue gold braid around jar lid.

6. Tie the bow and place on top of jar with mounting tape.

Jessica the Cat's Christmas Tale

Storyteller: This is Jessica, my cat. Jessica has lived in our house as long as I can remember. Jessica and I have shared many quiet times together and she has told me many wonderful things.

Jessica told me this story that she had heard from her great grandmother cat who was named Jesse.

Jesse lived long, long ago in a town called Nazareth. She belonged to a young girl named Mary. Mary was a gentle, kind girl who always gave Jesse milk from the family goat that she milked. Mary would brush Jesse's long, brown fur and make her feel very loved.

Mary grew up and married a man named Joseph. Joseph was a carpenter who built furniture and cabinets. He knew Mary loved Jesse and so he built a special box for Jesse to sleep in.

As time went by, Joseph and Mary had to take a trip to the town of Bethlehem to pay their taxes. Mary was going to have a baby and she was very sad about leaving her family. Joseph thought that she might not be so lonely if Jesse went with them to Bethlehem.

Joseph saddled the donkey and tied Jesse's special box onto the saddle. They traveled a long way and were very tired when they got to Bethlehem. Joseph went to many hotels, but all the rooms were filled. One kind man told Joseph that he and Mary could sleep in his barn that he had just put fresh, clean hay in.

Joseph helped Mary off the donkey and took Jesse's box down and they went into the barn. They spread their blankets on the fresh, clean hay so that they could sleep. They were very tired.

During the night Jesse awoke to the most wondrous sight. A bright star was shining over the barn and in the manger there was a new baby sleeping. Jesse asked the cow:

Jesse: "What has happened?"

Storyteller: The cow answered with a soft:

Cow: "Moooooo"

Storyteller: Jesse asked the donkey:

Jesse: "What has happened?"

Storyteller: The donkey replied in a most regal way:

Donkey: "Hee, Haw!"

Storyteller: Jesse asked the sheep:

Jesse: "What has happened?"

Storyteller: The sheep gave a soft:

Sheep: "Baa, baa."

Storyteller: Jesse asked the doves in the top of the barn:

Jesse: "What has happened?"

Storyteller: The doves fluttered their wings and sang:

Doves: "Coo-coo, Coo-coo."

Storyteller: Jesse heard beautiful singing and went to sit beside Mary. Mary looked down and smiled and said:

Mary: "Jesse, we now have a little boy named Jesus to look after and care for."

Storyteller: Jesse rubbed against Mary's leg and purred (*make a purring sound*). Now Jesse knew what had happened. A beautiful new baby had been born this night. When the shepherds came to the barn with their sheep and the wise kings came riding their camels Jesse smiled her best cat smile for she knew that on this special night the world had been truly blest.

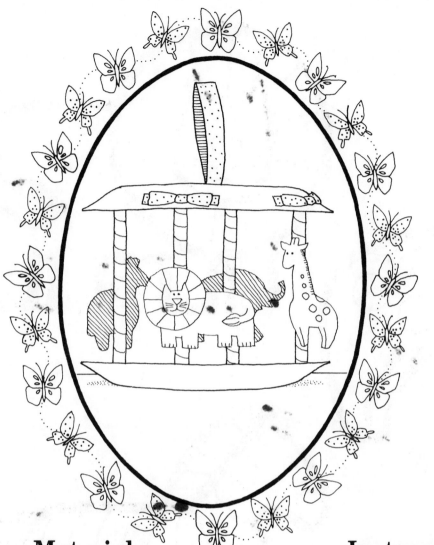

Merry-Go-Round

Materials

- Glue
- Scissors
- Crayons
- Paper punch
- Two paper plates or paper shallow bowls (small size—7 inches)
- Four drinking straws (paper straws adhere best to glue but plastic can be used), 6½ to 7½-inches long
- Four pieces of ribbon 10 inches long, ½-inch wide (4 little bows)
- One 14-inch long, ½-inch wide ribbon folded in half for handle

Instructions

1. Put two paper plates together and punch out four evenly spaced holes ½-inch from edge with paper punch.
2. Cut straws into four 7½-inch pieces. Split top and bottom of straw pieces to form flaps for gluing in place.
3. Glue straws into holes on paper plates, matching top and bottom holes. Allow to dry.
4. Glue on or staple ribbon for handle.
5. Color animals, cut them out and glue one animal onto each straw.
6. Tie 4 small bows with ribbon, and glue them near straw holes on top of Merry-Go-Round.

lion
(cut 1)

giraffe
(cut 1)

zebra
(cut 1)

elephant
(cut 1)

Nursery Crafts

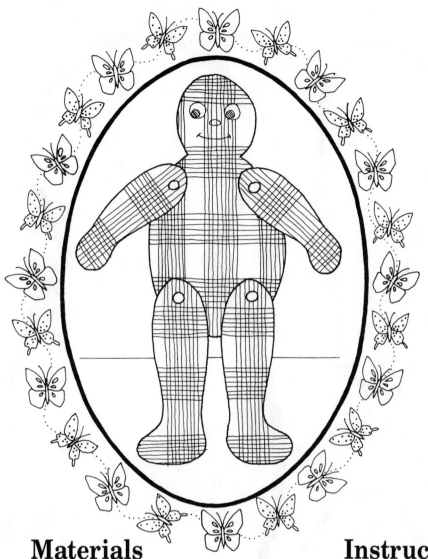

Moving Boy

Materials

- Glue
- Scissors
- Black marking pen
- Modge podge
- Brush for modge podge
- Black/white construction paper for eyes
- One piece of white poster board
- One 9 × 12-inch piece of orange checked material (orange and white gingham)
- Four brad fasteners

Instructions

1. Apply a coat of modge podge to the uncut poster board.
2. Lay the fabric on the board and smooth it out.
3. Apply a coat of modge podge to the top of material. Allow to dry.
4. Draw and cut out body patterns from the poster board.
5. Cut out pattern for eyes.
6. Attach arms and legs with brad fasteners.
7. Glue on eyes.
8. Use marking pen to make nose and mouth.

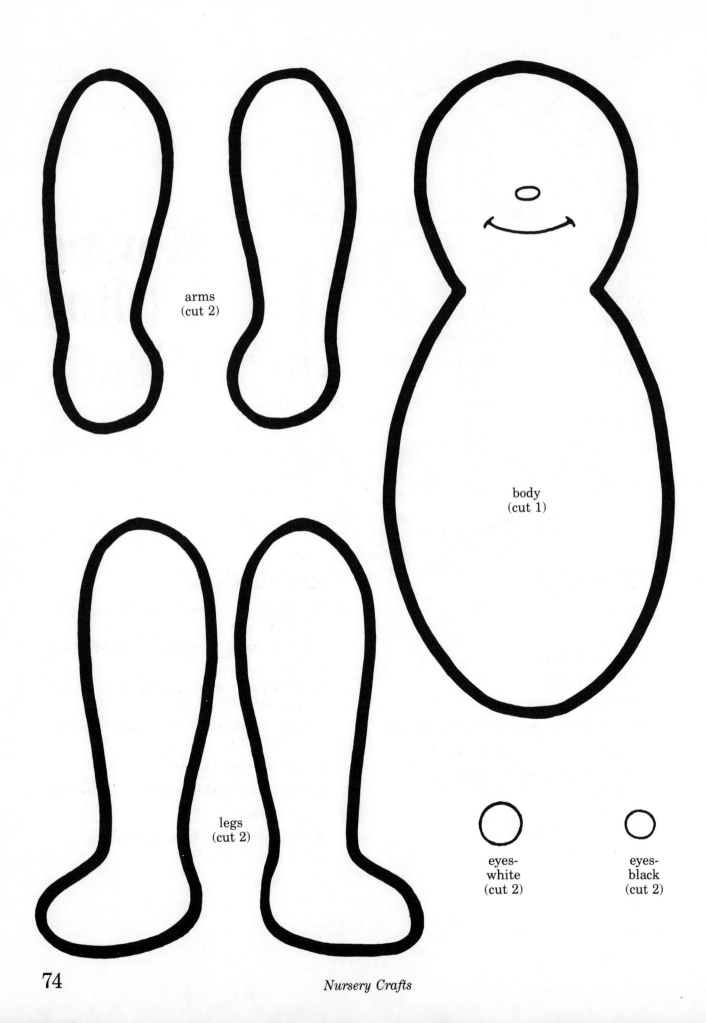

arms
(cut 2)

body
(cut 1)

legs
(cut 2)

eyes-
white
(cut 2)

eyes-
black
(cut 2)

Nursery Crafts

Nature Odds 'n' Ends

Materials

- Glue
- Water
- Sponge brush (can be purchased at hardware or hobby shop)
- Wood shavings or sawdust
- One small decorative mushroom (plastic or styrofoam)
- One small stick (twig)
- One small plastic flower
- Two little plastic mice or other animals
- One 7 × 4-inch heavy poster board or index card for base

Instructions

1. Using a slightly dampened sponge brush, spread glue evenly over the poster board or index card.

2. Spread the sawdust over this mixture.

3. Glue on the mushroom, twig, flower, and mice.

Odds 'n' Ends Glue On

Materials

- Glue
- Scissors
- Tape
- One 2-inch mirror
- One small thread spool
- One green pipe cleaner, cut in half
- Four dried flowers
- One small plastic mouse
- Two 2-inch squares of colored construction paper for flower and butterfly

Instructions

1. Glue the spool to the center of the mirror.
2. Cut out the butterfly and glue or tape to the pipe cleaner half.
3. Cut out the flower patterns, glue together, and glue or tape to the other pipe cleaner half.
4. Glue the mouse on the spool.
5. Place the pipecleaner flower, butterfly, and dried flowers inside the spool.

flower
center
(cut 1)

flower
petals
(cut 1)

butterfly
(cut 1)

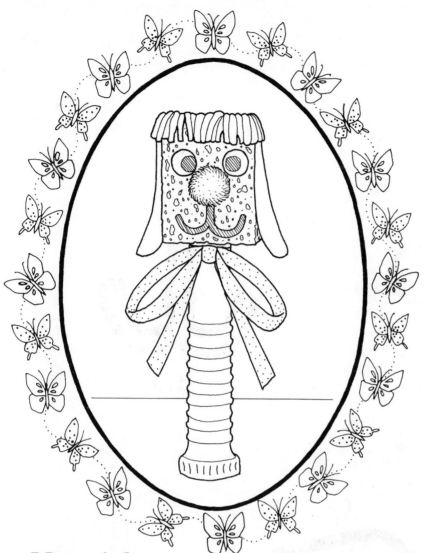

Old Bones

Materials

- Glue or glue gun

- Scissors

- Black/white construction paper for eyes

- Old sponge hose attachment (can be purchased at drug and hardware stores)

- One piece of brown fringe, 2½ inches long, for hair

- One 1-inch pom-pom for nose

- Black or brown construction paper for ears and mouth

- One ribbon, ¾-inch wide and 12-inches long, for bow

Instructions

1. Cut out patterns.

2. Glue eyes, nose, and mouth onto front of sponge.

3. Glue fringe onto top of sponge so that it hangs over forehead like hair.

4. Glue one ear to each side of sponge.

5. Tie ribbon around handle and make a bow.

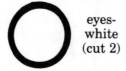 eyes-
white
(cut 2)

 mouth
(cut 1)

 eyes-
black
(cut 2)

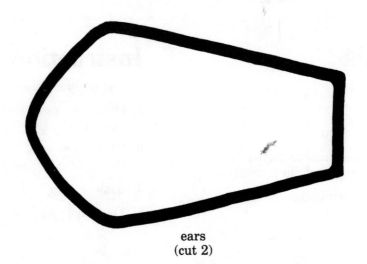 ears
(cut 2)

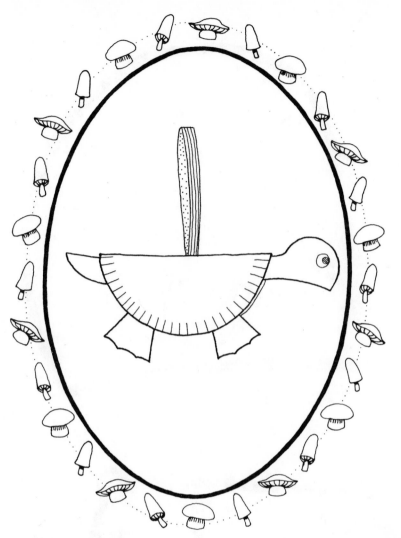

Paper Plate Turtle

Materials

- Glue
- Scissors
- Stapler
- Black/white construction paper for eyes
- One bright green paper plate, colored on both sides, for turtle body (can be purchased at party or import store)
- One brightly colored paper plate (other than green) for turtle shell
- One 12-inch long, ¾-inch wide ribbon for handle

Instructions

1. Cut out turtle body pattern pieces from green paper plate.

2. Fold paper plate for shell in half and staple together, leaving openings for feet, head, and tail.

3. Fold ribbon in half to make handle and staple to the top center of the turtle shell.

4. Slip the head, feet, and tail into the shell openings. Staple in place.

5. Cut out eyes and glue one onto each side of head.

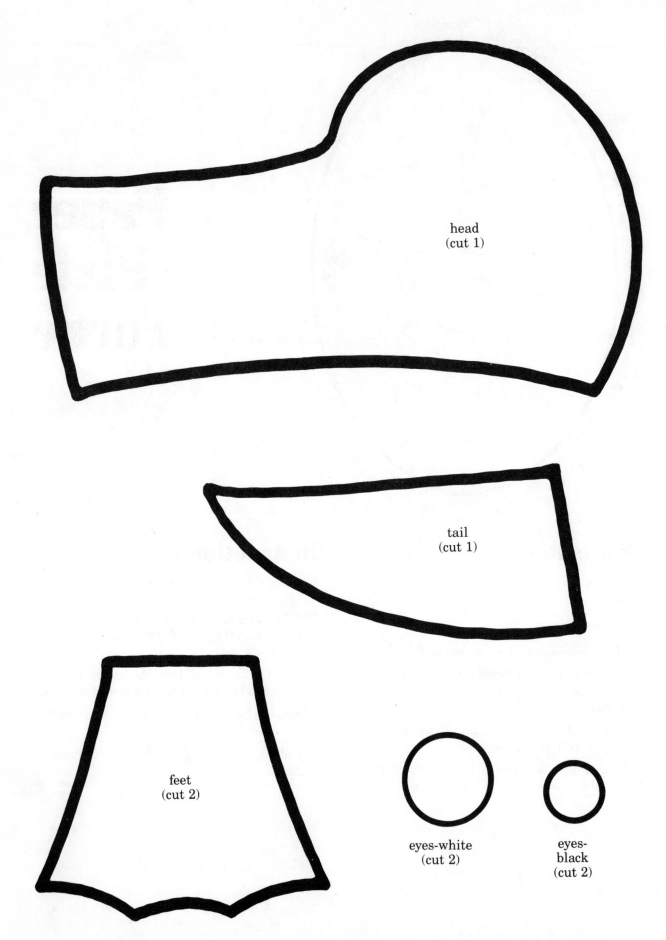

head
(cut 1)

tail
(cut 1)

feet
(cut 2)

eyes-white
(cut 2)

eyes-black
(cut 2)

Paper Sack Grandma Puppet

Materials

- Glue
- Scissors
- One lunch sack
- Quilt batting for hair
- Two 1-inch plastic moving eyes
- One piece of red construction paper for mouth
- One 1-inch black pom-pom for nose
- One 1-inch wide ribbon, 32 inches long, for bow

Instructions

1. Glue plastic moving eyes onto sack.
2. Cut out mouth from red construction paper and glue onto sack.
3. Glue on pom-pom for nose.
4. Glue on quilt batting for hair.
5. Using ribbon, tie a large bow and glue to top of hair.

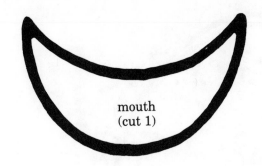

mouth
(cut 1)

Puppet Show Story
Grandmother's Mother's Day

This special mom is not only a mother, she is also a grand-mother.

Grandmother is going to have visitors today. She is expecting visits from her grandchildren and her children because it is MOTHER'S DAY today.

It's time! All the visitors arrive and they all have special gifts for Grandmother. Each one gives Grandmother a great big hug and a great big kiss.

They all share a special dinner and talk about special times they've all had together. They even share a few songs and open all of Grandmother's gifts. Ohhhh, what lovely things she has received.

"I have had such a wonderful day with you all," says Grand-mother, "and now I have a surprise for you that I have been saving all this time. Now you all must remember to be very quiet and follow me." Grandmother takes the group through the house to a door in the back, which is closed. Now what on earth could Grandmother be up to? Everyone is very curious about the surprise!

Grandmother turns and says, "Shhh, be quiet," to all of them and starts to open the door. It opens only a crack and, all of a sudden, out run twelve of the cutest little puppies that anyone had ever seen. They bark and bounce and lick and oh are they having a good time! "Yup, yup, yup," they bark.

Needless to say, Grandmother's old dog, Sweetheart, has quite a group of puppies, and she is being honored as a special mom too. Everyone enjoyed Grandmother's special Mother's Day surprise and the day that they spent at her house.

Nursery Crafts

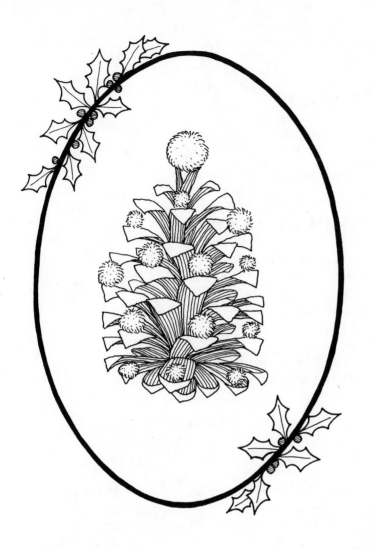

Pinecone Christmas Tree

Materials

- Glue
- One pinecone 3–4 inches tall, 2½-inches wide
- One 1-inch yellow pom-pom for top of tree ornament
- Six (or more) ¼-inch pom-poms of different colors
- Eight (or more) ½-inch pom-poms

Instructions

1. Glue various sized pom-poms onto pinecone petals.
2. Glue 1-inch pom-pom to top of pinecone.

Fingerplay
Christmas Trees

Christmas trees! Christmas trees!
How many do you see?
Christmas trees! Christmas trees!
Count them with me.
A tall one, (*thumb*)
A short one, (*index*)
And one that's so fine— (*middle*)
One of those three will surely be mine!

Pinecone Petal Turkey

Materials

- Glue or glue gun
- Scissors
- Straight pin
- Petals from pinecone (15 large petals for feathers, 3 small petals for underneath chin)
- Posterboard for head
- One plastic moving eye, ¼-inch wide
- One drinking straw cut in half for legs
- One ribbon, 8 inches long, ½-inch wide, for bow
- One cup hook
- One small wooden scrap board, approximately 3½ × 6 inches
- Wood stain or paint for scrap board
- Paint brush
- One 2½-inch styrofoam ball, cut in half

Instructions

1. Screw cup hook into top of board for hanging. Have the children stain or paint their wood piece. Let dry.

2. Glue the flat end of the styrofoam ball onto the center of the board.

3. Push the large pinecone petals into the ball, for tail feathers.

4. Glue ends of straws and push glued ends into ball for legs.

5. Cut out head and glue onto ball. Secure with a straight pin.

6. Glue on eye, and glue on small pinecone petals to back of head so that they hang down under chin.

7. Tie ribbon onto cup hook and make a bow.

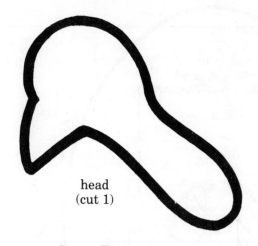

head
(cut 1)

Story Time

Bobby Joe's Thanksgiving Dinner

Storyteller: Once upon a time I knew a family. These are the people in the family. This is Grandma and Grandpa. Here are Mama, Daddy, and Aunt Em. These are the children. The big brother's name is C.W. The girls are Billie Sue and Peachy. The little brother is Bobby Joe. One night Grandma said:

Grandma: "Thanksgiving will be here before we know it. It's about time we started planning our Thanksgiving dinner. I'll bake the turkey and make the dressing. What will you do for Thanksgiving, Aunt Em?"

Aunt Em: "Well, I make mighty good rolls and cranberry sauce. Billie Sue, what about you?"

Billie Sue: "I could make some apple pies."

Storyteller: And Daddy said:

Daddy: "I had a mighty good crop of apples this year. I'll bring the apples for the apple pies."

Storyteller: And Mama said:

Mama: "I'll fix the vegetables. Let's see, we could have green peas, squash and sweet potatoes with marshmallows on the top. Grandpa, what will you do for Thanksgiving?"

Grandpa: "I'll bring in some wood and build a big fire in the fireplace. C.W., what about you?"

C.W.: "Well, we have a whole lot of pecans on the pecan tree. I'll fill up a big basket with pecans."

Nursery Crafts

Storyteller: Peachy said:

Peachy: "Well, I'm too little to cook, but I could set the table."

Storyteller: Little Bobby Joe had listened to everybody tell what they'd do for the Thanksgiving dinner, but he couldn't think of a thing to do. Then he had an idea. He said:

Bobby Joe: "What I can do is help everybody!"

Storyteller: Grandma said:

Grandma: "You'll be the best helper in the family, Bobby Joe."

Storyteller: So the family started getting ready for their Thanksgiving dinner. Grandma put the turkey in the oven and started on the dressing. Little Bobby Joe stood on a chair and helped Grandma crumble the cornbread for the dressing.

Then Daddy and Bobby Joe went down to the cellar to get the apples. Bobby Joe helped Daddy carry the apples upstairs.

Billie Sue made the apple pies and Bobby Joe sprinkled cinnamon and sugar on the apples. Aunt Em rolled out the dough for the rolls and Bobby Joe helped her cut them out and put them on the pans to rise.

Mama cooked the green peas and the squash and the sweet potatoes. Bobby Joe put marshmallows on top of the sweet potatoes.

Grandpa brought in the logs to make the fire in the fire-place. Bobby Joe brought in the kindling and crumpled up the paper to help the fire get started. C.W. took the big basket out in the yard to the pecan tree. Bobby Joe helped him fill it with pecans.

Peachy put the lace tablecloth on the table and then put out a plate for each person. While she put the forks and knives by the plates, Bobby Joe put a spoon by each plate.

The house smelled good with Thanksgiving cooking. Finally Grandma said:

Grandma: "The dinner is ready. Come sit down."

Storyteller: The family was hungry by now and they all sat down at the big table covered with the dinner they had all helped to make. They bowed their heads and they all held hands. Together they said:

Family: "We are thankful for our family and our good Thanksgiving dinner."

Storyteller: Then they ate the big Thanksgiving dinner they had all helped to make. Grandma was right. Little Bobby Joe was the very best helper in the family.

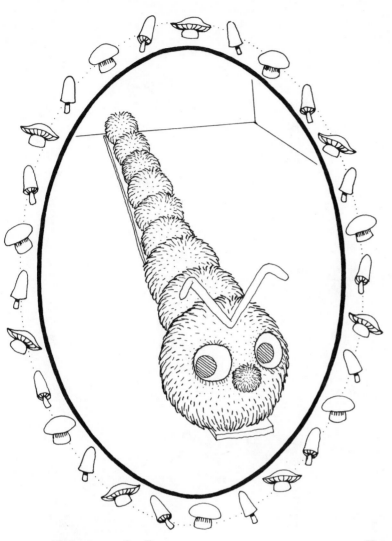

Pom-Pom Caterpillar

Materials

- Glue
- Scissors
- One 1½-inch bright pink pom-pom
- Two ¾-inch yellow pom-poms
- Six ½-inch pom-poms (assorted colors)
- One piece of pink felt, 5½ × ½-inches, for base
- One ¼-inch black pom-pom for nose
- One pipe cleaner cut to 3 inches long
- Two ½-inch plastic moving eyes

Instructions

1. Cut out felt pattern.
2. First glue large pom-pom head onto base, and then glue on progressively smaller sizes until finished.
3. Fold pipe cleaner in half, and glue on for antennas.
4. Glue on eyes and nose. Let dry.

(cut 1)

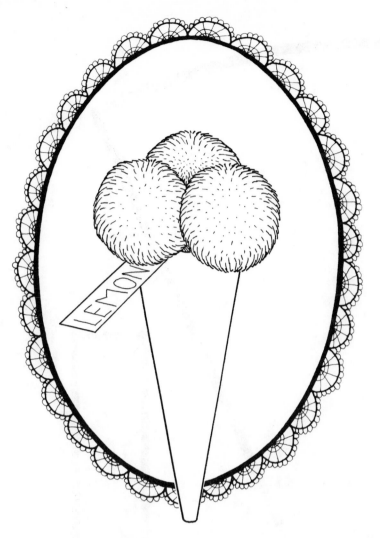

Pom-Pom Ice Cream Cone

Materials

- Glue
- Scissors
- Marking Pen
- Three 2-inch pom-poms in different colors; yellow for lemon ice-cream, brown for chcolate, etc.
- One piece of brown construction paper for cone
- One piece of white construction paper for label

Instructions

1. Cut out ice cream cone pattern.
2. Roll it up to make a cone.
3. Glue the seam; tape or staple it securely.
4. Glue the three pom-poms on top of the cone, each one next to another (not on top of each other).
5. Cut out small label.
6. Write the flavor of the ice cream on label and glue or staple on cone.

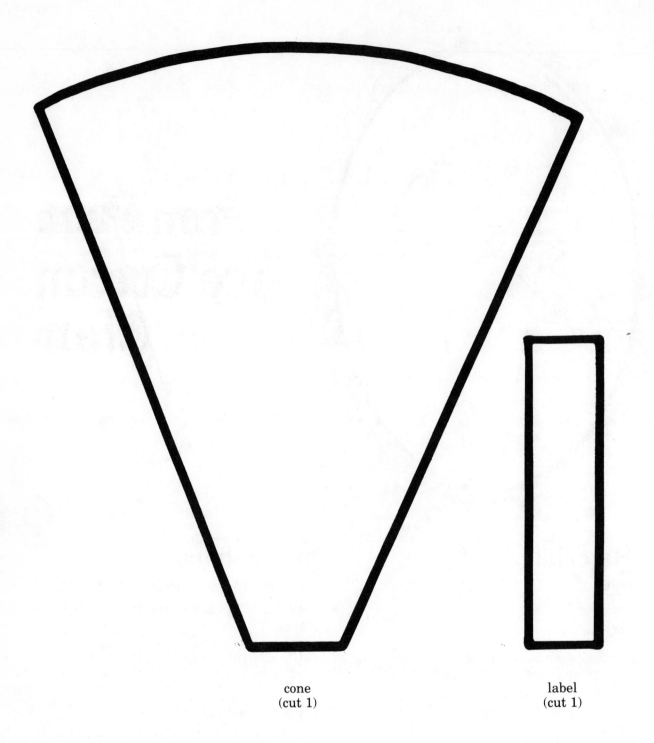

cone
(cut 1)

label
(cut 1)

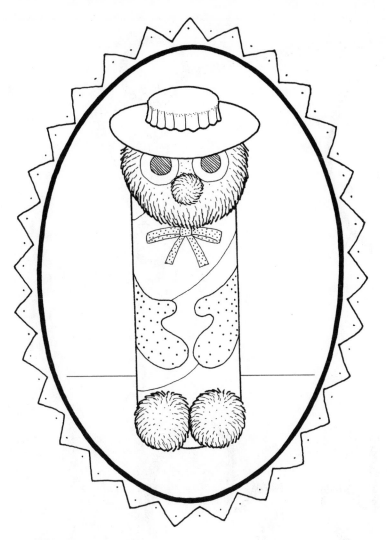

Pom-Pom Pioneer Man

Materials

- Glue
- Scissors
- Black/white construction paper for eyes
- One paper towel cylinder (cut to 4 inches long)
- One piece of construction paper for hat rim
- One 2-inch pom-pom for head
- One soda pop bottle cap for hat
- Two 1-inch pom-poms for feet
- One small, ½-inch pom-pom for nose
- One gingham ribbon, 3 inches wide, 6 inches long, for hands
- One 5-inch piece of ribbon, ⅛-inch wide, for bow tie

Instructions

1. Cut out hands from gingham ribbon.
2. Glue hands, feet, and pom-pom head onto paper cylinder body.
3. Glue eyes and nose on head.
4. Cut out hat rim from construction paper. Glue bottle cap onto hat rim.
5. Glue hat onto the head.
6. Make a bow out of ⅛-inch wide ribbon and glue it on for a bow tie.

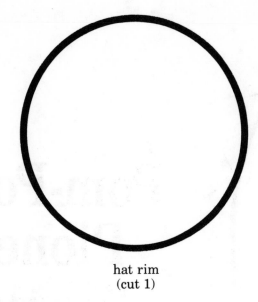

hat rim
(cut 1)

eyes-
white
(cut 2)

eyes-
black
(cut 2)

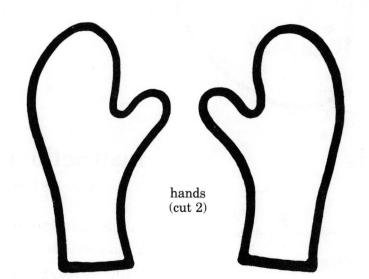

hands
(cut 2)

Pom-Pom Pioneer Woman

Materials

- Glue
- Scissors
- Tape or pin
- Black/white construction paper for eyes
- One paper cup
- One 2-inch pom-pom for head
- One small, ½-inch pom-pom for nose
- One piece of plaid scrap material for scarf
- One ribbon, 2 inches wide and 6 inches long, for hands

Instructions

1. Cut out hands from 2-inch ribbon and glue on upside down paper cup.
2. Glue on 2-inch pom-pom for the head.
3. Cut out eyes.
4. Glue on eyes and nose.
5. Glue scarf loosely around pom-pom head and secure with a pin or tape.

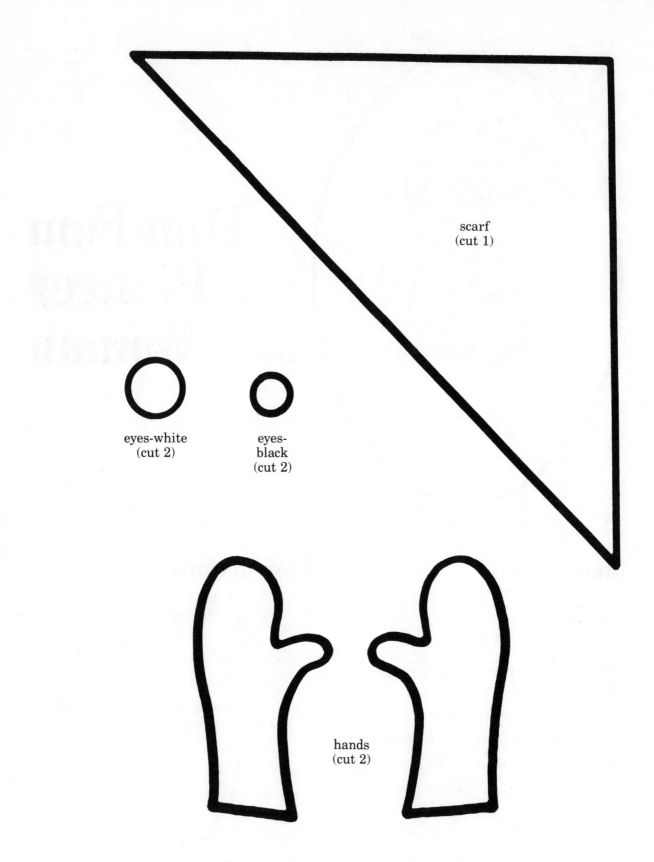

scarf
(cut 1)

eyes-white
(cut 2)

eyes-
black
(cut 2)

hands
(cut 2)

Pumpkin on a Stick

Materials

- Glue
- Scissors
- Stapler
- One piece of orange construction paper for pumpkin
- One piece of yellow construction paper for eyes, nose, and mouth
- One craft stick or tongue depressor (can be found in hobby stores)

Instructions

1. Cut out patterns.
2. Glue eyes, nose and mouth on pumpkin.
3. Staple the pumpkin to the craft stick.

mouth
(cut 1)

eyes
and
nose
(cut 3)

pumpkin
(cut 1)

Story Time
Winky Witch

Storyteller: Long, long ago and far, far away deep in the dark woods there was a scary cave. This was the cave where the witches lived.The old mean witches had long crooked noses with big warts on the ends. They had great big yellow teeth that made them look ugly when they laughed their scary laughs. They wore long black witch dresses and tall black witch hats.

Now, there was a tiny witch named Winky Witch who lived in the scary cave with the big mean witches. Winky Witch wore a long black witch dress, too, but it was too long and she always tripped on it. Her tall black witch hat was too big and it always fell down over her eyes. And, Winky Witch was not ugly. She couldn't scare anybody. She wasn't a good witch at all. She was even scared of the dark.

One dark, dark Halloween night the witches came out of their scary cave. They called their black cats and got out their big black pot. The witches put frog tails and fleas and spider webs into the pot. Then they danced around it, stirring it with a big spoon. They laughed their scary laugh.

Witches: (In a scary voice) "Ha, ha, ha, ha! Double bubble, double bubble. Tonight we'll make trouble. Ha, ha, ha, ha!"

Storyteller: Winky Witch danced around the pot with the big witches. She tried to laugh a scary laugh, too, but it sounded like this:

Winky Witch: (in a tiny voice) "Ha, ha, ha, ha! Double bubble, double bubble, Tonight we'll make trouble. Ha, ha, ha, ha!"

Storyteller: Then the witches called their black cats and jumped on their broomsticks and flew high up in the dark sky. Winky Witch flew on her little broomstick right behind the big witches. Soon the witches saw a bright light down on the ground below. They flew down close to the light.

It was a candle in a Jack O'Lantern. Then the witches played a trick! They blew out the Jack O'Lantern's candle just like this:

Witches: (Pretend to blow out the candle)

Storyteller: Then the witches laughed their scary laugh.

Witches: "Ha, ha, ha, ha! Double bubble, double bubble. Tonight we'll make trouble. Ha, ha, ha, ha."

Storyteller: The witches flew back up high in the dark sky to look for more Jack O'Lanterns. It got darker and darker and the big witches flew faster and faster. They flew too fast for little Winky Witch. Soon she was all alone in the dark sky. Winky Witch was scared. Just then she saw a bright light far down on the ground. She said:

Winky Witch: "I'll fly down there where it's not dark."

Storyteller: When she got near the light, Winky Witch saw it was a Jack O'Lantern. She stood up as tall as she could and tried to look mean like the big witches so she could scare the Jack O'Lantern.

Winky Witch: (in a tiny voice) "Ha, ha, ha, ha! Double bubble, double bubble. Tonight I'll make trouble. I'm going to blow out your candle."

Storyteller: Just as she was about to blow out the Jack O'Lantern's candle, her tall black witch hat fell down over her eyes and she tripped over her long black witch dress and she fell right down. The Jack O'Lantern wasn't scared a bit. He laughed and said:

Jack O'Lantern: (in a deep voice) "Ho, ho, ho, little witch. If you play a trick on me and blow out my candle it will be dark."

Storyteller: Winky Witch was scared of the dark and she didn't really want to blow out the nice Jack O'Lantern's candle.

Winky Witch: "I am a witch and witches are supposed to play tricks on Halloween. What can I do if I don't blow out your candle?"

Storyteller: The Jack O'Lantern said:

Jack O'Lantern: "You can go trick or treating with me and the children will give us candy. I will light up the dark for you with my candle!"

Storyteller: And that's just what they did. When you go trick or treating on Halloween night, if you look really hard, you just may see Winky Witch and the Jack O'Lantern.

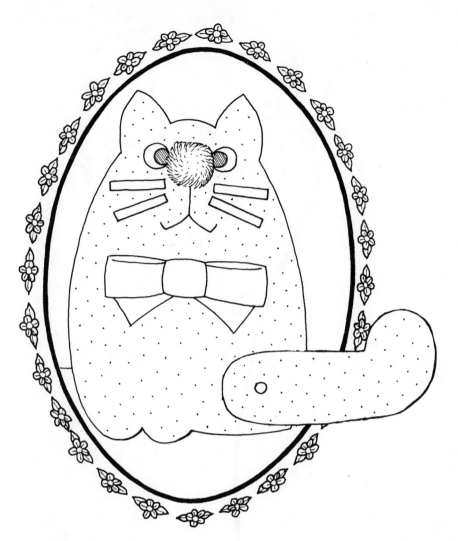

Pussy Cat

Materials

- Glue
- Scissors
- Black marking pen
- One piece of posterboard
- One 1-inch black pom-pom for nose
- Eighteen inches of 1-inch wide black satin ribbon, for bow and whiskers
- One piece of scrap fabric
- One brass brad fastener
- Black/white construction paper for eyes

Instructions

1. Cut out the pattern pieces from posterboard.
2. Glue the scrap fabric on posterboard and cut around edges to fit.
3. Cut ribbon into two pieces: one 15-½ inches long, and one 2-½ inches long.
4. Make a bow with the long piece of ribbon and glue onto cat's body.
5. Cut short piece of ribbon into ¼-inch widths and glue on for whiskers.
6. Glue on pom-pom nose, and eyes.
7. Draw mouth with marking pen.
8. Use the brad fastener to attach the tail to body. (You may wish to use a paper punch to make a hole first.)

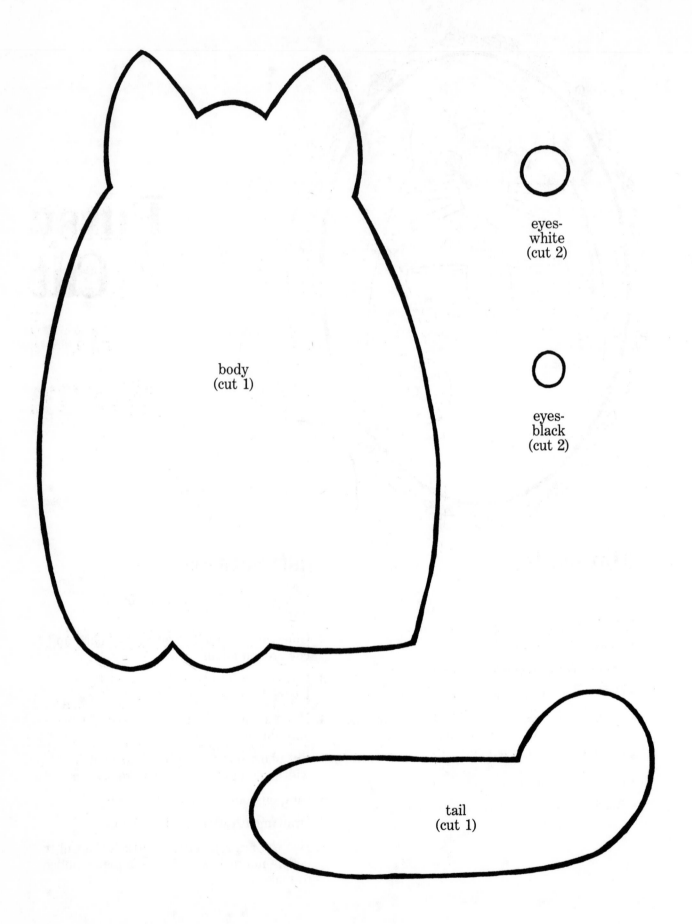

body
(cut 1)

eyes-
white
(cut 2)

eyes-
black
(cut 2)

tail
(cut 1)

Red Apple and Worm

Materials

- Glue
- Scissors
- One piece of red construction paper for apple
- One piece of green construction paper for stem
- One green pipe cleaner, cut in half, for worm
- One 1-inch pom-pom for head
- One ¼-inch pom-pom for nose
- Two ¼-inch plastic moving eyes

Instructions

1. Cut out patterns.
2. Glue stem on apple.
3. Roll the pipe cleaner around a pencil and make a small, tight spring for the worm's body.
4. Glue on the pom-pom for the worm's head, and then glue on the eyes and nose. Allow to dry.
5. Glue the pipe cleaner worm onto the apple and allow to dry.

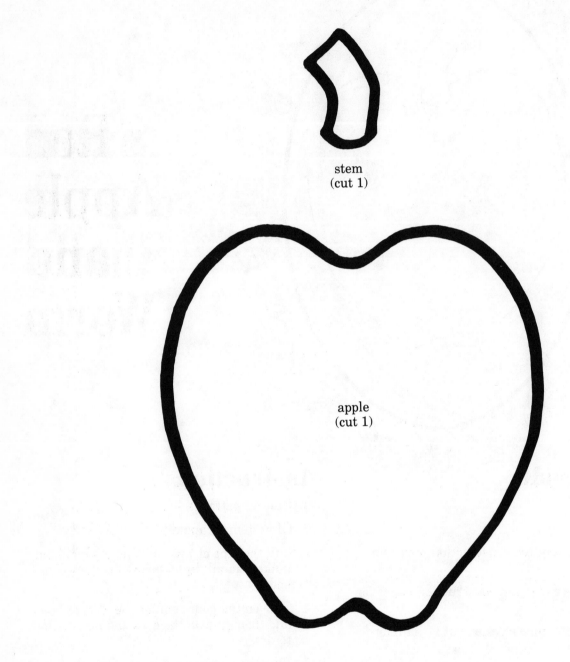

stem
(cut 1)

apple
(cut 1)

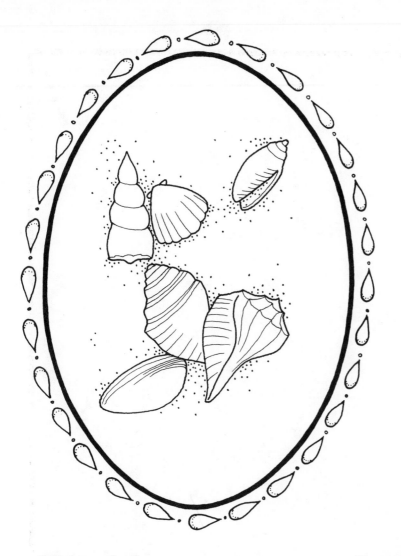

Sand and Shells

Materials

- Glue
- Water
- Sponge brush
- One piece of blue poster board for base
- Six small shells
- Sand

Instructions

1. Using a slightly dampened sponge brush, spread glue evenly over the poster board.

2. Sprinkle sand over the glue, and shake excess off.

3. Glue the shells onto the paper.

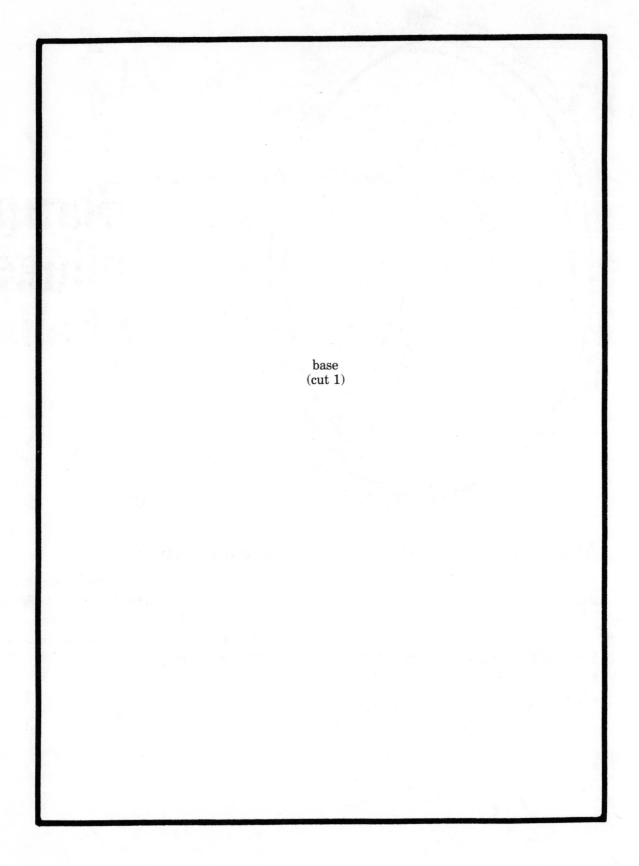

base
(cut 1)

Nursery Crafts

Scrap Collage

Materials

- Glue

- One piece of construction paper, bright color, cut in circle (Paper plates are also fun to use.)

- Scraps left over from other projects: yarn, ribbon, string, buttons, rickrack, cotton balls, straws, bottlecaps, sticks, stickers, macaroni, etc.

Instructions

1. Cover the circle with bits of glue.

2. Spread all scrap materials in the center of the table.

3. Tell the children to pick their pieces and glue them on.

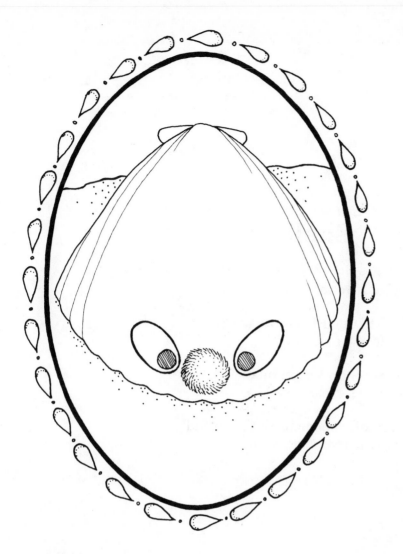

Sea Shell Creature

Materials

- Glue
- One medium-sized sea shell
- One ½-inch pom-pom for nose
- Two small plastic, moveable eyes (oval)

Instructions

1. Glue eyes in place on sea shell.
2. Glue nose on sea shell.

Children's Rhyme
Shells

I found a seashell at the shore,
And held it to my ear

I thought I heard the ocean roar,
As I held it near.

And now when I remember
My summer at the sea,

My seashell echoes back the sound
In pleasant memory.

Skywriter

Materials

- Glue
- Scissors
- One piece of colored posterboard for airplane
- One piece of white posterboard for propeller
- One brass brad fastener
- One yard ⅛-inch wide ribbon
- One piece of scrap fabric

Instructions

1. Using pattern, cut airplane from colored posterboard.
2. Cut propeller from white posterboard.
3. Glue fabric to propeller. Cut around edges to fit.
4. Attach propeller to airplane using brass brad fastener. (You may want to first punch a hole with a paper punch.)
5. Cut ribbon to four 9-inch lengths, and attach to back of airplane, as illustrated.

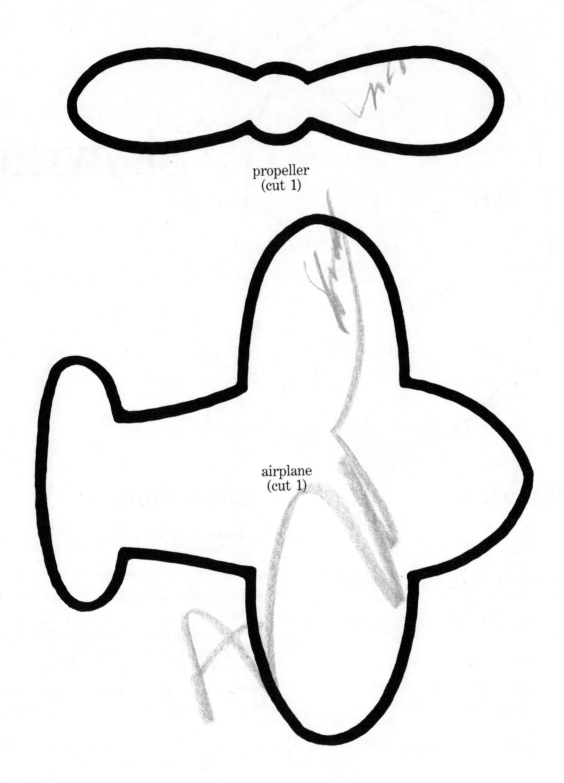

propeller
(cut 1)

airplane
(cut 1)

Nursery Crafts

Snowman

Materials

- Glue
- Scissors
- One piece of white construction paper for snowman body and eyes
- One piece of black construction paper for eyes, nose, mouth, hat, and buttons
- One piece of red construction paper for hat band
- Three brad fasteners
- One ¼-inch wide paint stick or dowel, 12–15 inches long; if using a dowel, cut a 36-inch dowel into three sections

Instructions

1. Cut out pattern pieces.
2. Glue on facial features and buttons.
3. Glue on red hat band.
4. Attach hat and arms with brad fasteners.
5. Glue dowel or paint stick on the back, extending it about 9 inches up the snowman for a handle.

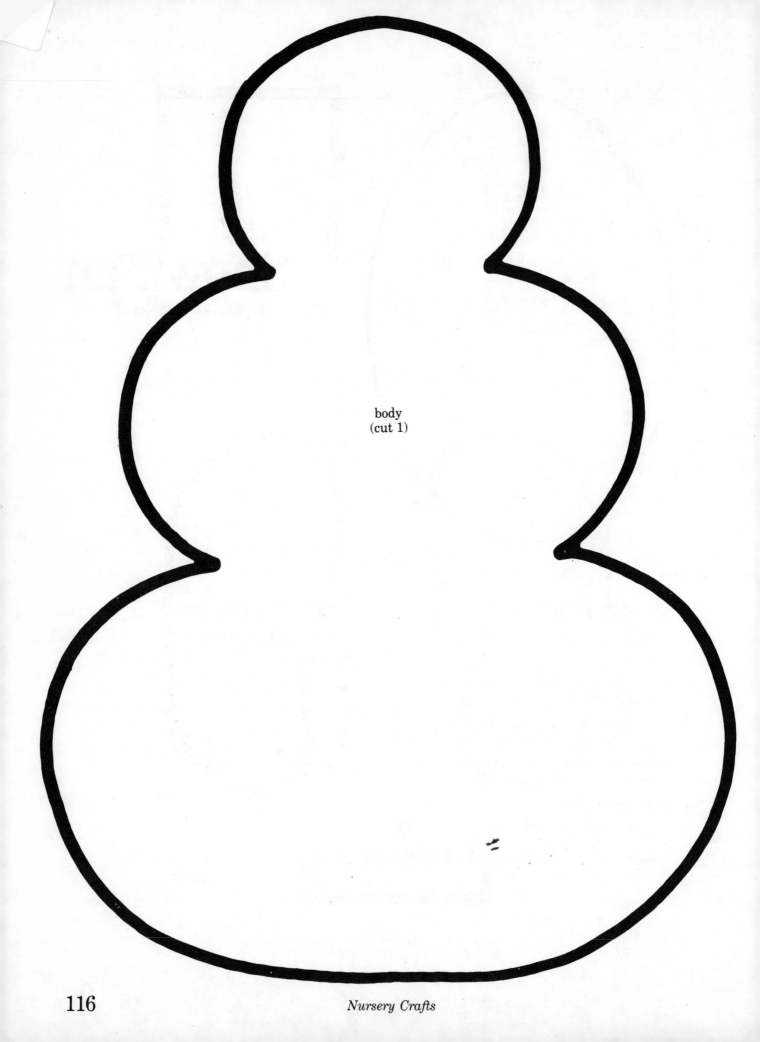

body
(cut 1)

Nursery Crafts

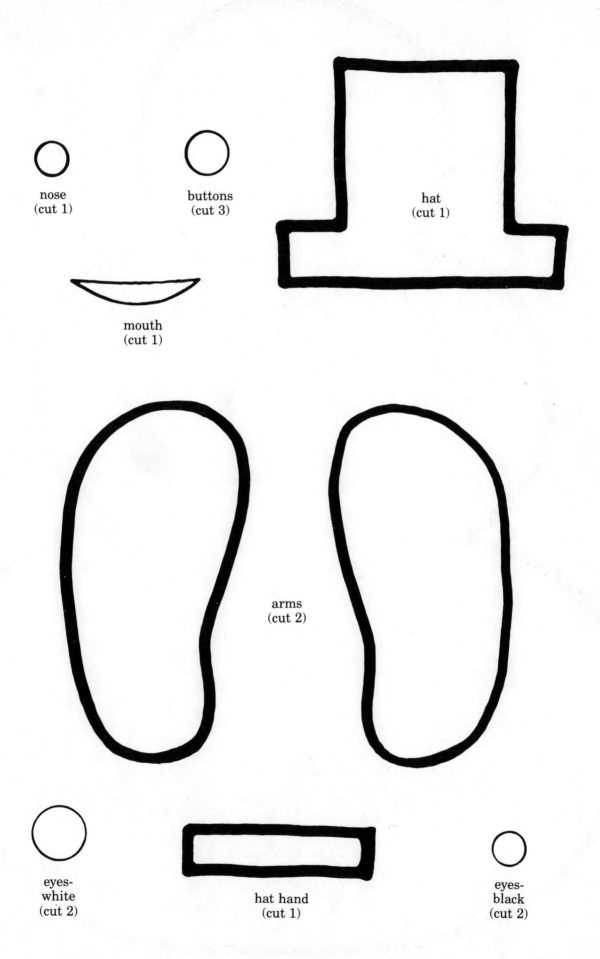

nose
(cut 1)

buttons
(cut 3)

hat
(cut 1)

mouth
(cut 1)

arms
(cut 2)

eyes-
white
(cut 2)

hat hand
(cut 1)

eyes-
black
(cut 2)

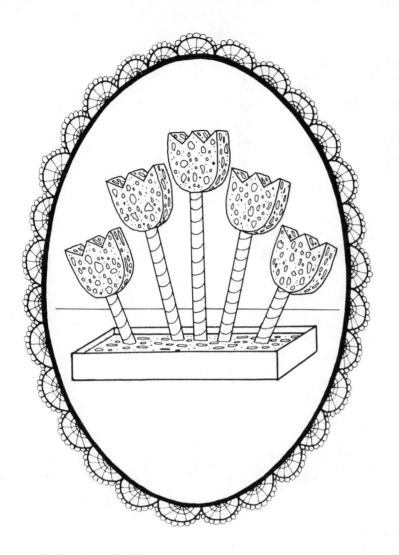

Sponge Tulips

Materials

- Glue or glue gun
- Scissors
- One brightly colored sponge (approximately 6 × 4 × ¾ inches) for tulips
- One green sponge (approximately 6 × 4 × ½-inches) for grass
- One box lid cut to 6 × 4 inches (a shoe box top works well)
- Five plastic straws
- Sharpened pencils

Instructions

1. Cut tulips out of sponge.

2. Create a small hole in bottom of each flower by puncturing sponge with the sharp pencil. Fill holes with glue, and insert straws for stems.

3. Glue the green sponge inside box lid, for grass.

4. Make five small holes in green sponge, using sharp pencil. Fill holes with glue, and insert tulip stems.

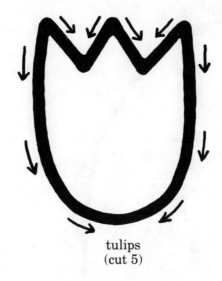

tulips
(cut 5)

First cut a small square, then cut out
two "v"'s, and then round out the bottom.

Children's Rhyme
Tulips

Red tulips, yellow tulips, rainbow colors too.
You lift your heads
In my flower beds,
And say, "How do you do?"

Sun Bonnet Puppet

Materials

- Glue

- Scissors

- Jar lid, approximately 2¼-inch wide

- Two plastic moving eyes, ¼-inch wide

- Acrylic paint: red, cheeks, nose and mouth; skin color, face (*If your students are very young and cannot paint, make the face out of construction paper and marking pen.*)

- Paint brush

- One piece of lace, ½-yard long, ½-inch wide, for bonnet decoration

- One piece of colored construction paper for bonnet circle and bonnet shade

- Ribbon, ½-yard long, ¼-inch wide, for bow

- Tongue depressor or small flat stick

Instructions

1. Cut out pattern pieces.

2. Paint or glue face on inside of jar lid. Glue on eyes.

3. Glue lace around edge of bonnet circle, and along curved edge of bonnet shade.

4. Glue bonnet circle to back of jar lid, bottoms touching. Glue stick to back of bonnet and lid. Let dry.

5. Glue flat side of bonnet shade to upper edge of jar lid. Hold in place till dry.

6. Run a thin line of glue all around edge of jar lid.

7. Place center of ribbon at top of lid edge, wrap ribbon around edge, and secure at bottom with a knot. Make a bow.

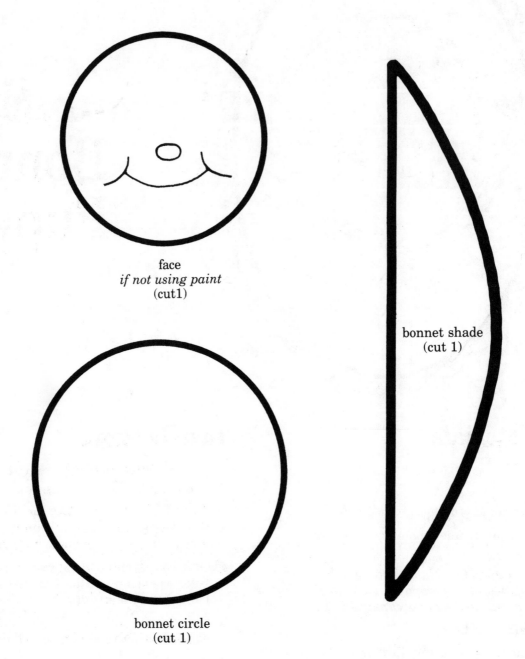

face
if not using paint
(cut1)

bonnet shade
(cut 1)

bonnet circle
(cut 1)

Sunshine

Materials

- Glue
- Scissors
- Black marking pen
- Black/white construction paper for eyes
- One felt square, bright yellow, for large sunrays
- One piece of orange construction paper for small sunrays
- One 16-inch long, ¾-inch wide ribbon for handle
- One piece of pale yellow felt for face

Instructions

1. Using bright yellow felt, cut out the large rays of sun.
2. Cut the circle for the face out of pale yellow felt.
3. Cut the smaller rays of sun out of the orange construction paper.
4. Cut out pattern for eyes.
5. Glue or staple on the ribbon handle.
6. Glue on the orange sun rays to the large yellow felt sun rays.
7. Glue on the yellow face. Glue on the eyes, and make a smile for the mouth with the marking pen.

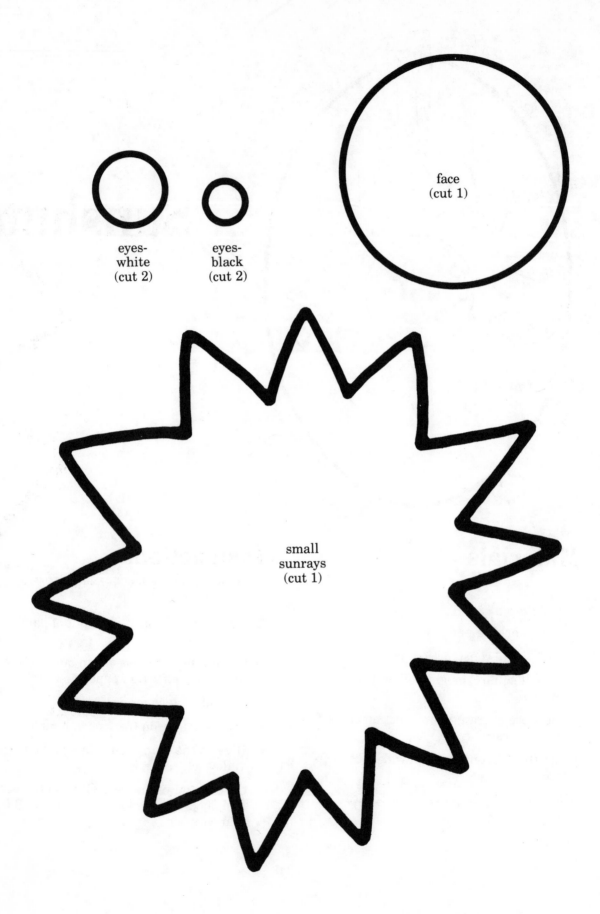

eyes-
white
(cut 2)

eyes-
black
(cut 2)

face
(cut 1)

small
sunrays
(cut 1)

124

Nursery Crafts

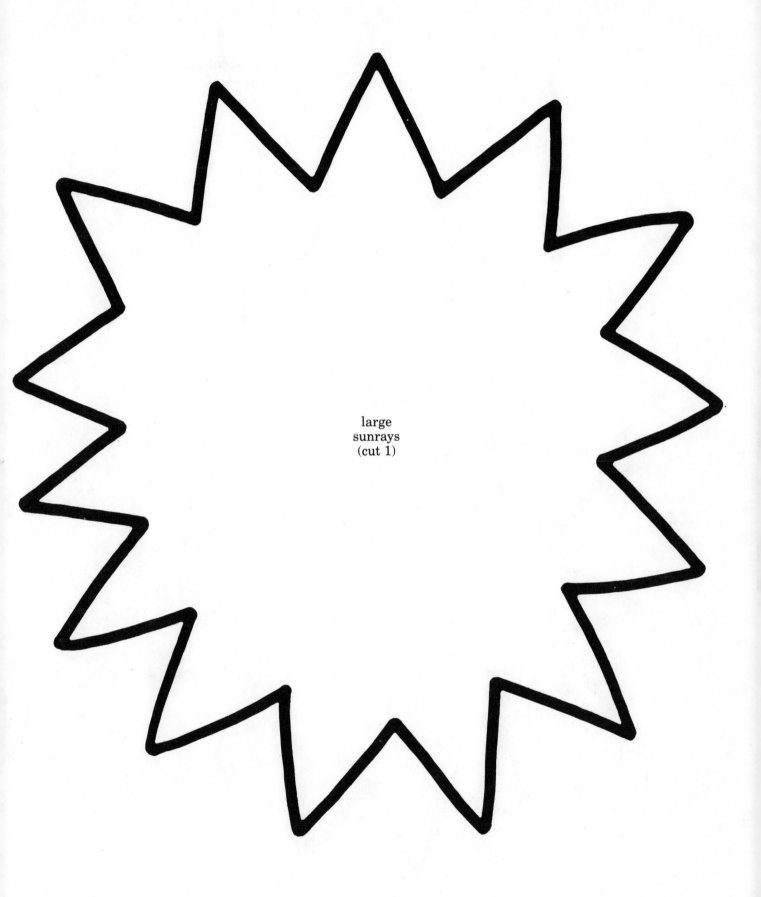

large
sunrays
(cut 1)

Suzy Duck

Materials

- Glue
- Scissors
- Orange crayon or thick marking pen
- One piece of yellow posterboard
- One brass brad fastener
- One piece of scrap material for wing and bow
- Black/white construction paper for eyes

Instructions

1. Cut out the duck body and wing from posterboard.

2. Glue a piece of fabric on the wing and cut around edges to fit.

3. Stick the brass brad fastener through the wing and body of the duck, so that the wing can move easily. (You may wish to use a paper punch to make a hole first.)

4. Make a ribbon from leftover material, and tie a bow. Glue to duck's head.

5. Glue eyes onto duck's face.

6. Color beak with crayon or marking pen.

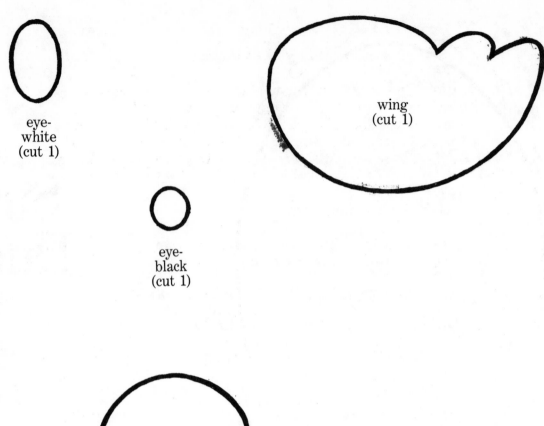

eye-
white
(cut 1)

wing
(cut 1)

eye-
black
(cut 1)

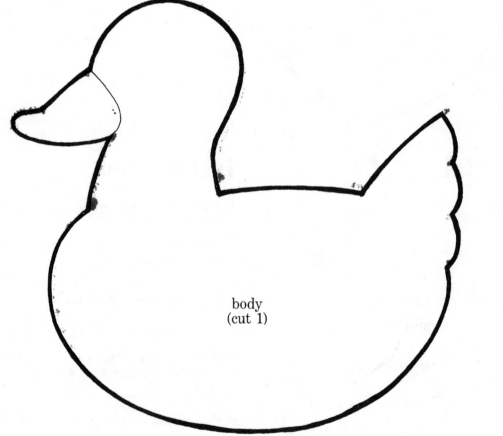

body
(cut 1)

Baby Duck

Storyteller: One bright sunny morning Mama Duck took the brand new Baby Duck for a walk to see the big world.

Mama Duck walked fast. Baby Duck toddled along behind her. Baby Duck stopped to smell the pretty flowers and Mama Duck went on over a big hill. When Baby Duck looked up, Mama Duck was gone. He called his Mama in his teeny tiny voice.

Baby Duck: "Quack, quack, quack."

Storyteller: But Mama Duck didn't come. So Baby Duck walked on until he met Brother Pig. He said:

Baby Duck: "Please, Brother Pig, will you call my Mama?"

Storyteller: Brother Pig said he'd be glad to call Baby Duck's Mama and he said:

Brother Pig: "Oink, oink, oink."

Storyteller: But Mama Duck didn't come. So Baby Duck walked on until he met Brother Rooster.

Baby Duck: "Please, Brother Rooster, will you call my Mama?"

Storyteller: Brother Rooster said he'd be glad to call Baby Duck's Mama and he said:

Brother Rooster: "Cockle-doodle-do."

Storyteller: But Mama Duck didn't come. So Baby Duck walked on until he met Sister Sheep.

Baby Duck: "Please, Sister Sheep, will you call my Mama?"

Storyteller: Sister Sheep said she'd be glad to call Baby Duck's Mama and she said:

Sister Sheep: "Baa, baa, baa."

Storyteller: But Mama Duck didn't come. So Baby Duck walked on until he met Sister Cow.

Baby Duck: Please, Sister Cow, will you call my Mama?"

Storyteller: Sister Cow said she'd be glad to call Baby Duck's Mama and she said:

Sister Cow: "Moo, moo, moo."

Storyteller: But Mama Duck didn't come. So Baby Duck walked on until he met great big Duncan Duck.

Baby Duck: "Please sir, Duncan Duck, will you call my Mama?"

Storyteller: Great big Duncan Duck said he'd be glad to call Baby Duck's Mama, and he said in his great big duck voice:

Duncan Duck: "Quack, quack, quack!"

Storyteller: And this time Mama Duck came running back over the hill to the little Baby Duck.

The Wheels on the Truck Go Round And Round

Materials

- Glue or glue gun
- Tape
- Scissors
- Two brad fasteners
- One piece of red poster board for truck
- One piece of black poster board for wheels
- One 1½-inch pom-pom for head
- Two plastic moving eyes, ¼-inch wide
- One straw, cut to approximately 3 inches, for neck
- One ¾-inch pom-pom for hood ornament

Instructions

1. Cut out pattern for truck and wheels from poster board. Cut window out of truck.
2. Use brad fasteners to attach the wheels to the truck.
3. Glue the large pom-pom to the straw, and glue on eyes.
4. Tape the straw to the back of the truck so that it looks like the little man is looking through the window.
5. Glue the other pom-pom on the hood of the truck. Let dry.

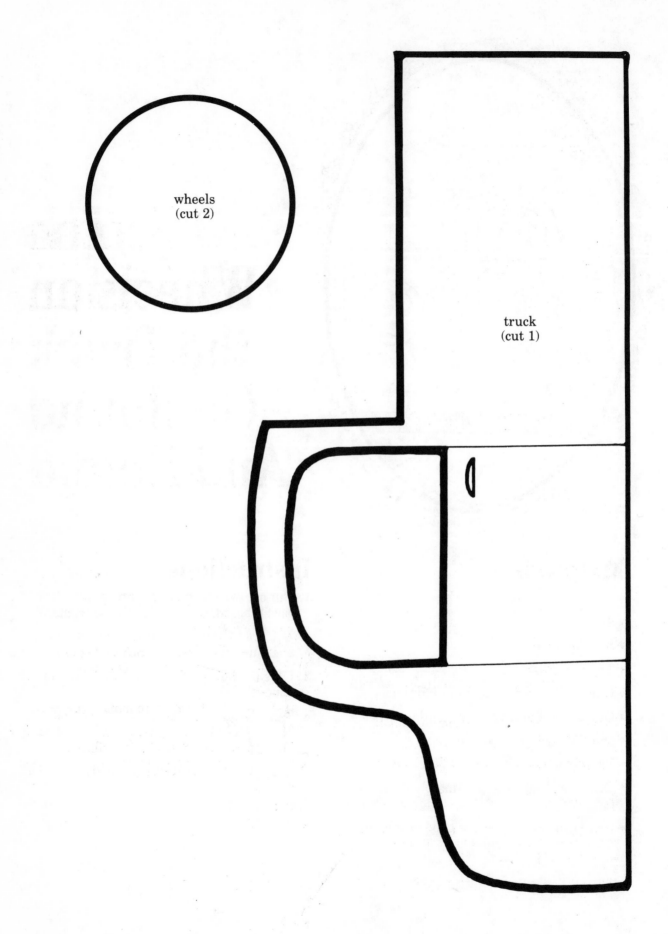

wheels
(cut 2)

truck
(cut 1)

Nursery Crafts

3-D Scotch Snowman

Materials

- Glue
- Scissors
- Black marking pen
- One package or roll of mounting tape (a thick, sticky tape that has adhesive on both sides)
- One piece of colored construction paper for background
- One piece of black construction paper for hat
- One piece of white construction paper for snowman
- One piece of Scotch plaid ribbon 1-inch wide, for bottom border
- One 9½-inch long, ½-inch wide Scotch plaid ribbon for tie

Instructions

1. Cut out snowman pieces and, using mounting tape, adhere to the background construction paper.

2. Using 9½-inch long, ½-inch wide plaid ribbon, tie a bow and glue it to the snowman.

3. Use black marking pen to make eyes, nose, and mouth.

4. Glue 1-inch wide Scotch plaid ribbon to bottom of background for border.

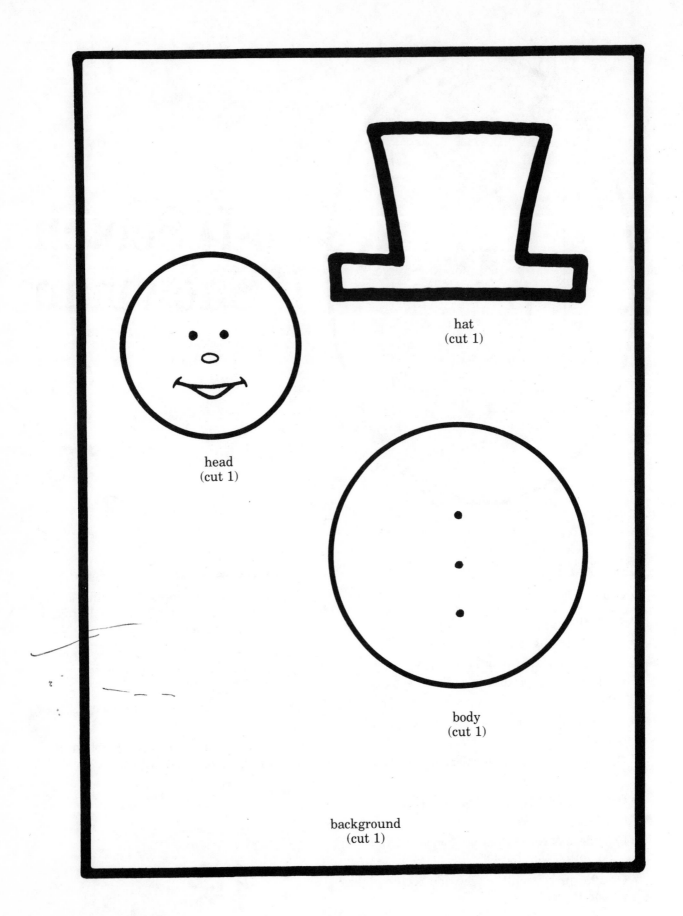

hat
(cut 1)

head
(cut 1)

body
(cut 1)

background
(cut 1)

Fingerplay
Five Fat Snowmen

Five fat snowmen were knocking at my door. (*hold up
     five fingers*)
This one melted, and then there were four. (*thumb down*)
Four fat snowmen were playing with me;
One more melted, and then there were three. (*index down*)
Three fat snowmen want to play with you,
But the next began to melt and that left two. (*middle down*)
Two fat snowmen, before the day was done,
Another one melted and then there was one! (*ring down*)
One fat snowman stayed out in the sun—
Silly, fat snowman! Now there are none! (*pinky down*)

Tool Box and Tools

Materials

- Glue
- Scissors
- Pinking shears
- Stapler
- Marking pen
- Black/white construction paper for eyes and mouths
- Four different colors of construction paper for tools
- One large piece of red construction paper for tool box
- One piece of brown construction paper for label

Instructions

Note: *Tools can be made from plain white construction paper and children can color them.*

1. To make tool box, fold red paper in half and staple sides together, leaving the top open.

2. Cut out label pattern and glue onto front of tool box. Write "Tool Box" on label with marking pen.

3. Cut out tool patterns, using pinking shears for saw edge.

4. Cut out eyes and mouths and glue onto each tool.

5. Place tools in toolbox.

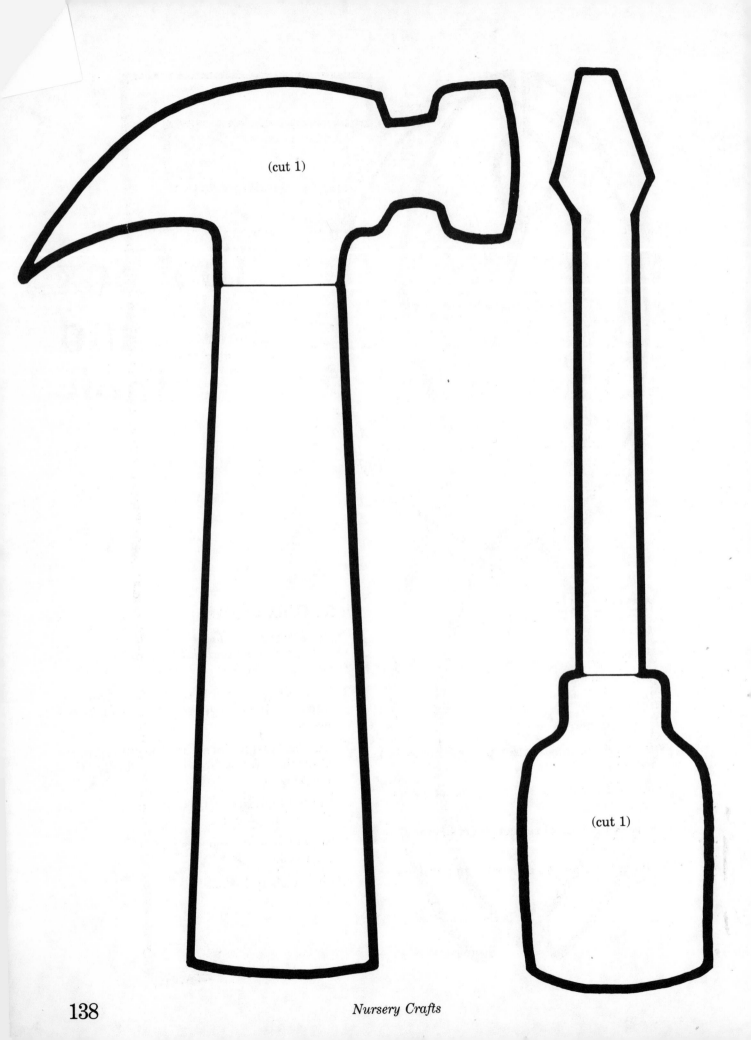

(cut 1)

(cut 1)

Nursery Crafts

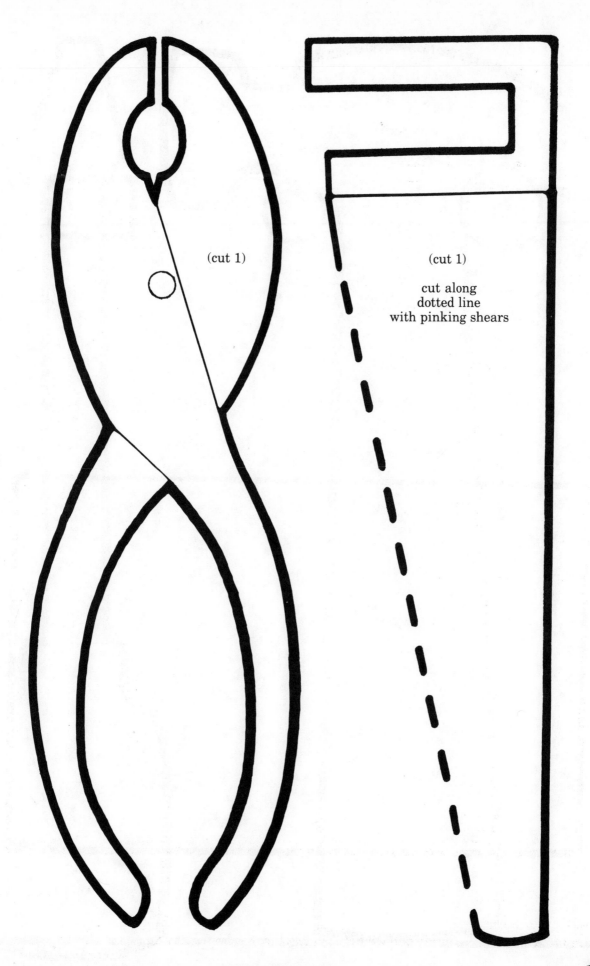

(cut 1)

(cut 1)

cut along
dotted line
with pinking shears

eyes-white
(cut 8)

eyes-
black
(cut 8)

mouths
(cut 4)

label
(cut 1)

(cut 1)

Valentine

Materials

- Glue
- Scissors
- Marking pen
- One piece of red construction paper for large heart
- One piece of white construction paper for small heart
- One 24-inch piece of lace
- One 4-inch long, 1½-inch wide red velvet ribbon (fold in half) for handle
- One 2-inch round mirror

Instructions

1. Cut out heart patterns.
2. Glue small heart on large heart.
3. Glue lace all around the back of the large heart.
4. Staple or glue the handle on and glue on the mirror.
5. Write "I LOVE YOU" on heart.

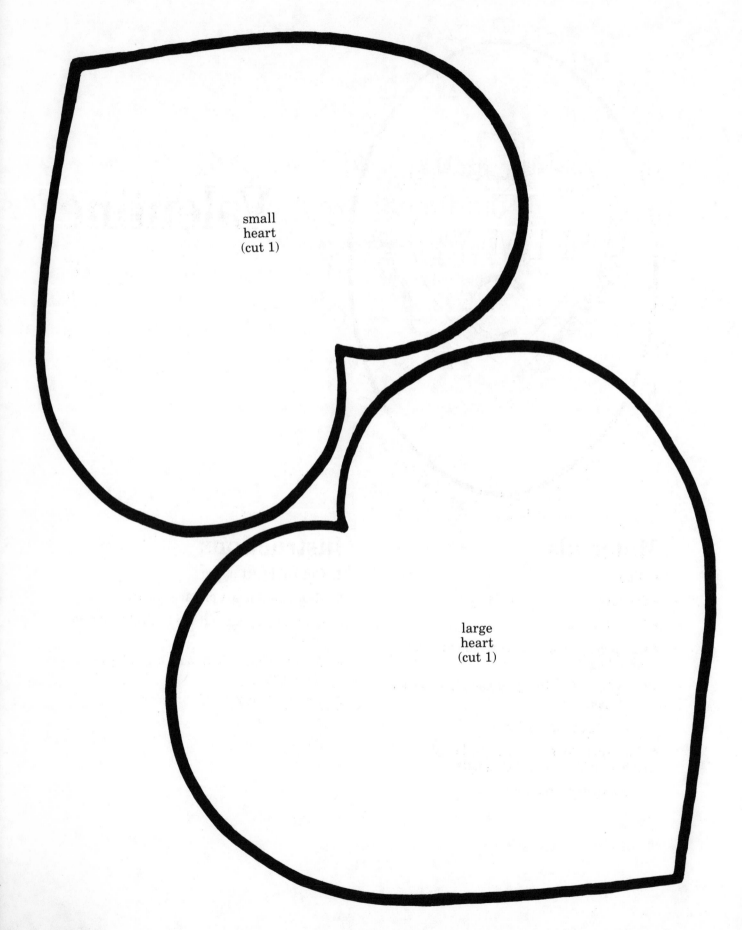

small
heart
(cut 1)

large
heart
(cut 1)

Children's Rhyme
Handprint Valentine

Here are my little handprints,
Especially for you.
They make a pretty valentine,
And say, "I love you" too!

Vegetable Basket

Materials

- Stapler
- Glue
- Scissors
- Crayons
- One piece old wallpaper (some stores give old wallpaper books away) for basket and handle
- One piece of white construction paper for vegetables
- Marking pen

Instructions

1. Cut out basket pattern, cutting along solid lines and folding along dotted lines. Draw details on vegetables with marking pen. Fold Tab A and Tab B behind Tab C, and glue together.

2. Cut out handle and staple to basket, matching dots on pattern pieces.

3. Color vegetables, cut them out and place in the basket.

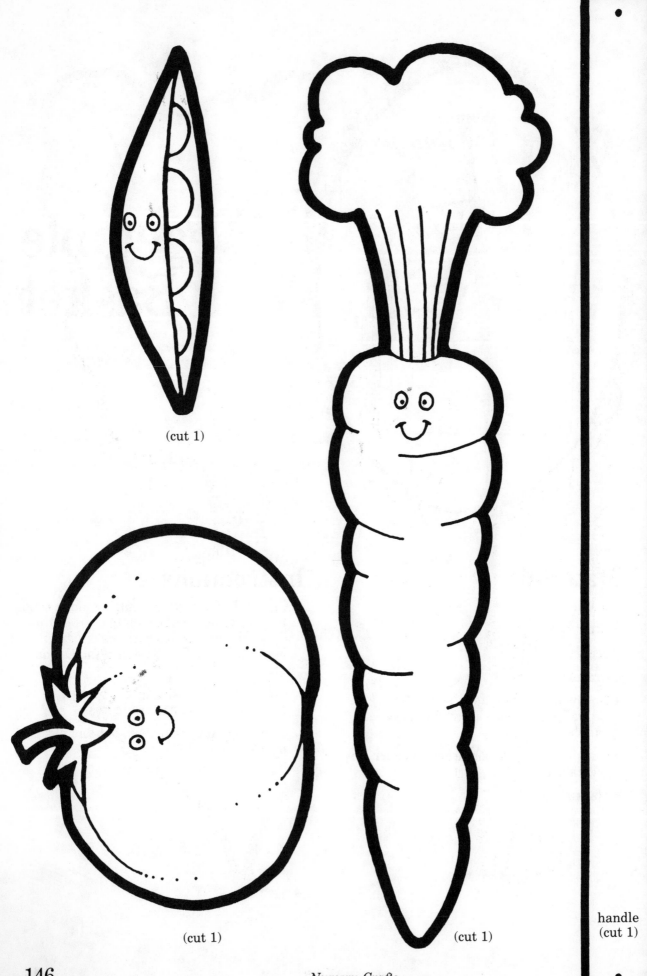

(cut 1)

(cut 1)

(cut 1)

handle
(cut 1)

146

Nursery Crafts

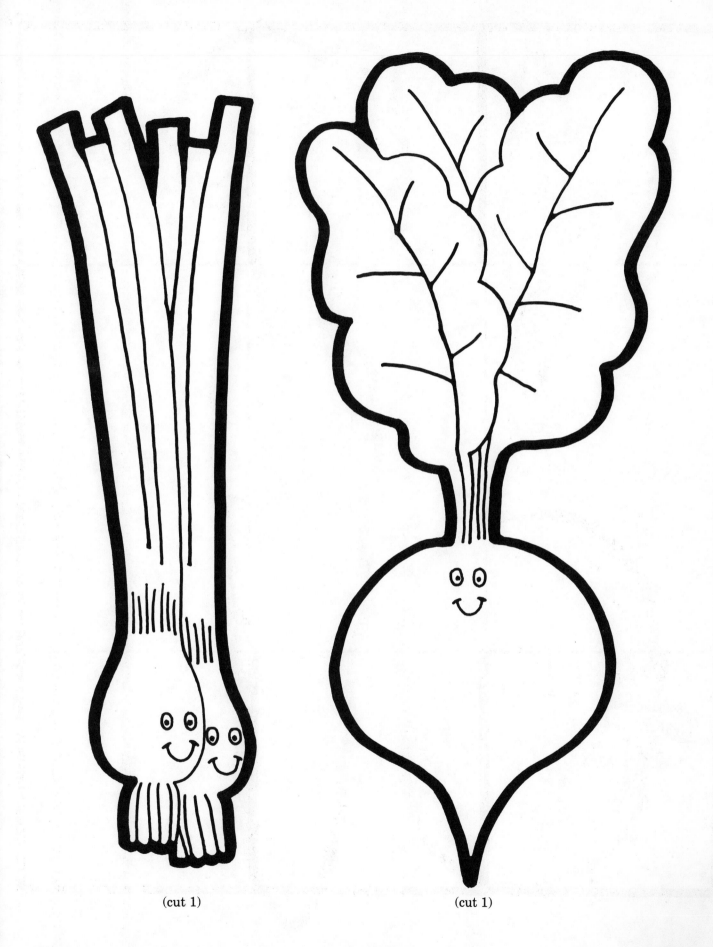

(cut 1)   (cut 1)

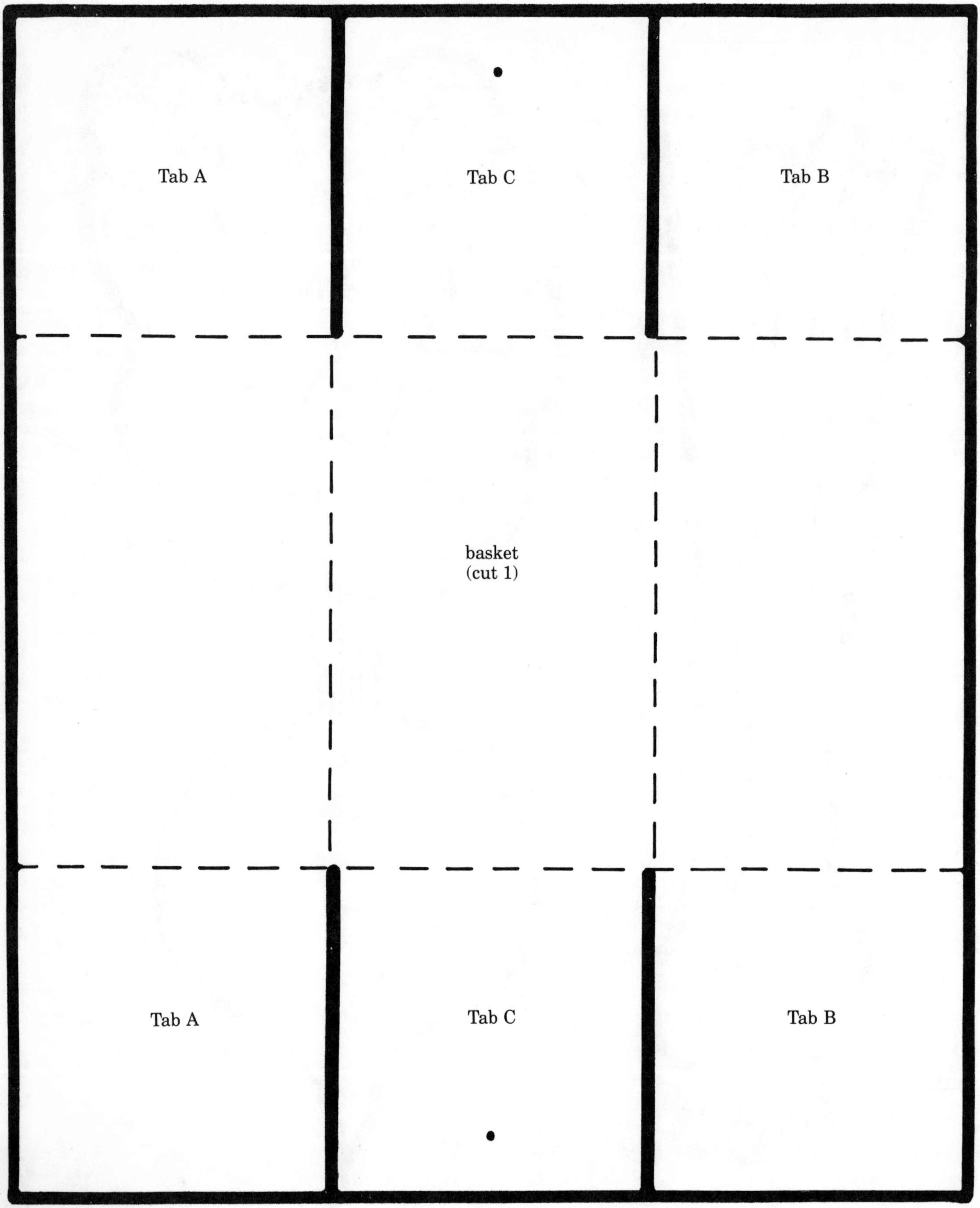

Tab A

Tab C

Tab B

basket
(cut 1)

Tab A

Tab C

Tab B

Children's Rhyme
Vegetables

I always eat my vegetables,
Carrots and broccoli too.
My mother says they'll help me grow:
"Eat them, they're good for you!"
But there is just one vegetable
I can't seem to eat:
I don't care if I ever grow
If I have to eat a beet!

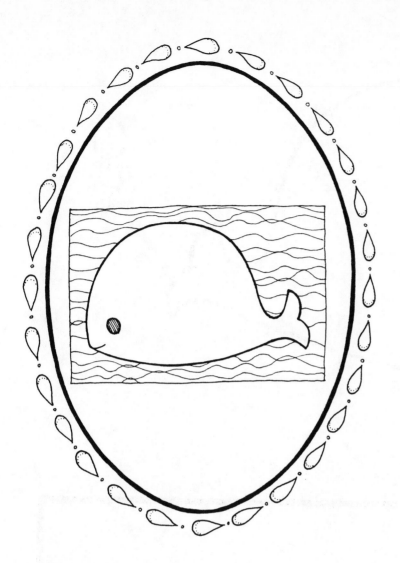

Wallpaper Fish

Materials

- Glue
- Scissors
- One piece of textured wallpaper for background, preferably blue to look like water
- One piece of white construction paper for fish
- Black construction paper for eyes
- Crayons

Instructions

1. Cut a 6-inch by 4-inch piece of wallpaper for the background.
2. Cut fish from white construction paper.
3. Cut out eyes and glue onto fish.
4. Glue fish onto wallpaper background.
5. Have the children color the fish.

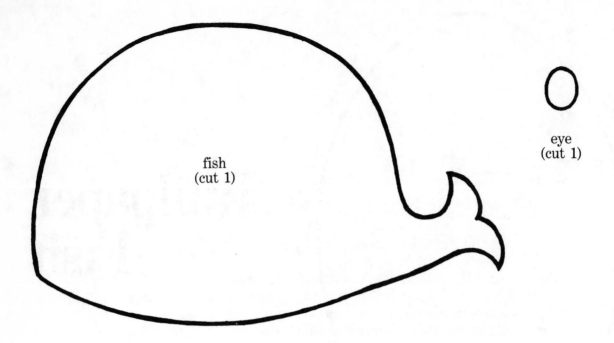

fish
(cut 1)

eye
(cut 1)

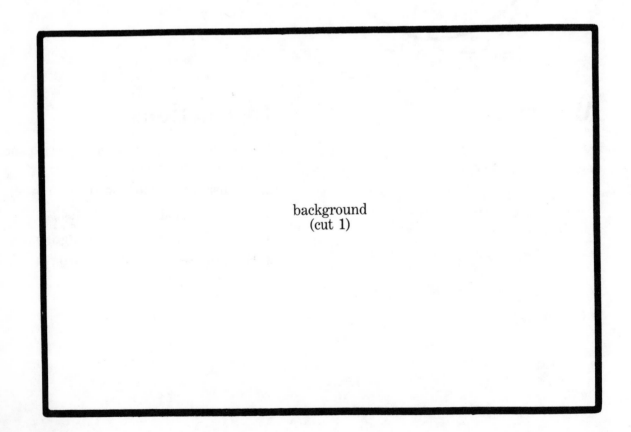

background
(cut 1)

Nursery Crafts

Children's Rhyme
Schools for Fish

In the Fish School, they don't learn
How to read or wait their turn;
And they don't learn one and one make two,
And they don't learn to paint or glue.
They never have to sit up straight,
Or be quiet or divide by eight.
They do pretty much just as they wish—
I think I'll join that school for fish!

Walnut Turtle

Materials

- Glue
- Scissors
- One half of a walnut shell
- One piece of green felt for turtle's body
- Two plastic moving eyes, ¼-inch or smaller

Instructions

1. Cut out the turtle's body.
2. Glue the walnut shell to the body.
3. Glue on the eyes.

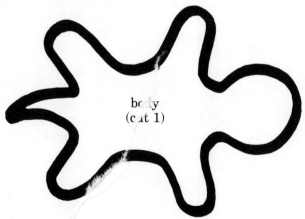

body
(cut 1)

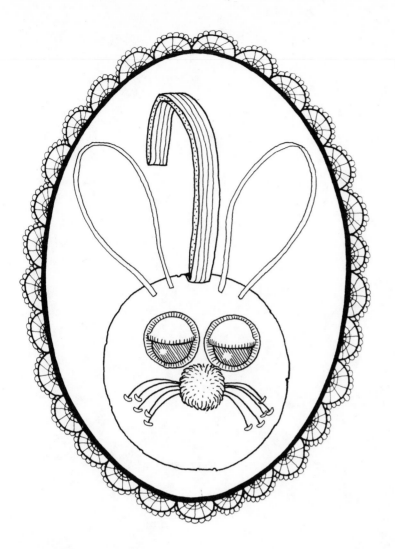

What-a-Rabbit

Materials

- Glue
- Scissors
- Pin
- One styrofoam ball (3 or 4-inch diameter)
- Two yellow, pink, or other color pipe cleaners for ears
- One white pipe cleaner cut in six equal lengths for whiskers.
- Two sleepy eyes (can be purchased at hobby shop)
- One 1-inch pink pom-pom for nose
- One 14-inch long, ½-inch wide ribbon for handle

Instructions

1. Place a small amount of glue on sleepy eyes and punch them into the styrofoam ball.

2. Glue pom-pom nose onto styrofoam ball.

3. Bend pipecleaners in half, shape them into ears, and push them into the styrofoam.

4. Glue pipe cleaners to each side of nose to form whiskers.

5. Fold ribbon in half and glue onto top of rabbit to form handle. Secure with pin.

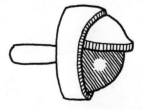

side view of sleepy eye

Who Who Who Feather Owl

Materials

- Glue
- Scissors
- Black marking pen
- Black/white construction paper for eyes
- One package of feathers
- One piece of brown construction paper for owl body

Instructions

1. Cut out patterns.
2. With the marking pen, draw the nose and feet of the owl.
3. Glue the feathers upside down on the front and back of the body. Allow to dry.
4. Glue heads to front and back of body, covering feather ends.
5. Glue eyes together. Draw circles around blacks of eyes.
6. Glue eyes on head.

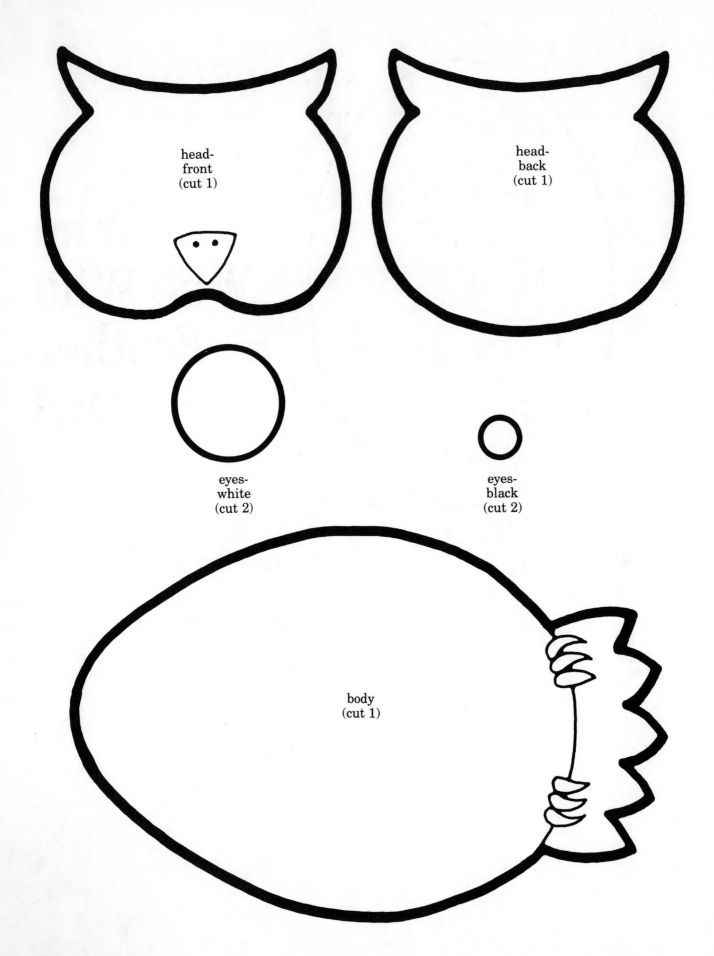

head-
front
(cut 1)

head-
back
(cut 1)

eyes-
white
(cut 2)

eyes-
black
(cut 2)

body
(cut 1)

Nursery Crafts

Bibliography

Caballero, Jane A. Ph.D. *Art Projects for Young Children,* Atlanta: Humanics Limited, 1979.

Carpenter, Sharan Bryant. *Scissor Sorcery,* Atlanta: Humanics Limited, 1985.

Graham, Terry Lynne. *Fingerplays and Rhymes,* Atlanta: Humanics Limited, 1984.

Taylor, Frances S. and Gloria Vaughn. *The Flannel Board Storybook,* Atlanta: Humanics Limited, 1986.

Humanics Publications

PARENT INVOLVEMENT

AVIATION & SPACE EDUCATION: Folder Games
Guaranteed to grab and hold the interest of children and increase awareness of our space program, these activities enhance skills in reading, writing, math, science, and social studies.

087-1   **$14.95**

READING RESOURCE BOOK
This excellent, highly readable text gives you an overview of children's language development, suggestions for games that enhance reading skills, ideas for establishing a reading environment in the home, tips for grandparents, and lists of resources.

HL-044-8   **$16.95**

WORKING TOGETHER:
A Guide to Parent Involvement
Ideal guide for those wishing to launch a new parent involvement program or improve existing parent/school communication and interaction. Favorably reviewed by the National Association for Young Children.

HL-002-2   **$16.95**

PARENTS AND TEACHERS
An intelligent, effective and field-tested program for improving the working relationship between parents and teachers. Now being used successfully in educational settings across the country.

HL-050-2   **$12.95**

ASSESSMENT

THE LOLLIPOP TEST
A Diagnostic Screening Test of School Readiness
Based on the latest research in school readiness, this test effectively measures children's readiness strengths and weaknesses. Included is all you need to give, score and interpret the test.

HL-028-6   (Specimen Set)   **$29.95**

THE PRESCHOOL ASSESSMENT HANDBOOK
Combines vital child development concepts into one integrated system of child observation and assessment. This is also the user's guide to the Humanics National Child Assessment Form — Ages 3 to 6.

HL-097-9   **$17.95**

THE INFANT/TODDLER ASSESSMENT HANDBOOK
User's guide to the Humanics National Child Assessment Form — Ages 0 to 3. Integrates crucial concepts of child development into one effective system of observation and assessment.

HL-049-9   **$15.95**

SOCIAL SERVICES

HUMANICS LIMITED SYSTEM FOR RECORD KEEPING
Designed to meet **all** record-keeping needs of family-oriented social service agencies, this guide integrates the child, family, social worker and community into one coherent network. Also the user's guide to proper use of Humanics Limited Record Keeping Forms.

HL-027-8   **$12.95**

REAL TALK:
Exercises in Friendship and Helping Skills
Real Talk teaches students basic skills in interpersonal relationships through such methods as role-playing and modeling. An ideal human relations course for elementary, junior high and high schools.

Teachers's Manual	HL-026-X	$ 7.95
Student's Manual	HL-025-1	$12.95

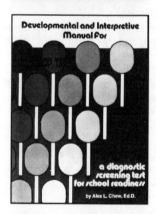

ORDER TOLL FREE
1-800-874-8844

HUMANICS LEARNING

P.O. Box 7447
Atlanta, Georgia 30309
(404) 874-2176

Humanics Publications

CHILDREN AROUND THE WORLD
Introduce preschool and kindergarten children to people and ways of other cultures.
HL-033-2   **$16.95**

THE FLANNELBOARD STORYBOOK
Step-by-step directions, story-telling techniques and how to make flannelboards and materials.
HL-093-6   **$16.95**

BIRTHDAYS: A CELEBRATION
More than 30 party themes and 200 games and activites are adaptable for children ages 3–10.
HL-075-8   **$14.95**

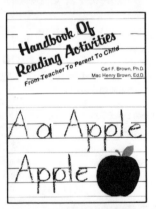

TEDDY BEARS AT SCHOOL
Learning center activities centered around teddy bears includes math, fine and gross motor skills, self concept and more. Ages 4–7
HL-092-8   **$16.95**

HANDBOOK OF READING ACTIVITIES
An innovative program used by teachers to involve parents with their children's beginning reading.
HL-036-7   **$12.95**

CAN PIAGET COOK?
Forty-six lesson plans with reproducible worksheets. Children experience science first hand with these food-related activities.
HL-078-2   **$12.95**

SCISSOR SORCERY
Over 50 reproducible, developmentally sequenced activity sheets help children learn to cut proficiently.
HL-076-6   **$16.95**

THE INFANT & TODDLER HANDBOOK
Activities for children birth to 24 months. For teachers, day care personnel, parents & other care givers.
HL-038-3   **$12.95**

TODDLERS LEARN BY DOING
Hundreds of activities are developmentally designed just for toddlers.
HL-085-5   **$12.95**

NUTS AND BOLTS
Guidelines for setting up an early learning center, organization and management.
HL-063-4   **$ 8.95**

THE CHILD CARE INVENTORY & MANUAL
Developed for infant & preschool programs. The Inventory reviews II performance areas. The manual explains how to collect, score and interpret the data.
HL-090-1   (Set) **$19.95**

HUMANICS LEARNING

The Successful Teacher's Most Valuable Resource!

EDUCATION

THE EARLI PROGRAM
Excellent language development program! Volume I contains developmentally sequenced lessons in verbal receptive language; Volume II, expressive language. Use as a primary, supplemental or rehabilitative language program.

Volume I	HL-067-7	$14.95
Volume II	HL-074-X	$14.95

LEARNING ENVIRONMENTS FOR CHILDREN
A practical manual for creating efficient, pleasant and stressfree learning environments for children centers. Make the best possible use of your center's space!

HL-065-0 $12.95

COMPETENCIES:
A Self-Study Guide to Teaching Competencies in Early Childhood Education
This comprehensive guide is ideal for evaluating or improving your competency in early childhood education or preparing for the CDA credential.

HL-024-3 $14.95

LOOKING AT CHILDREN:
Field Experiences in Child Study
A series of fourteen units made up of structured exercises dealing with such issues as language development, play and moral development in children. A fresh new approach to learning materials for early childhood educators.

HL-001-4 $14.95

YOUNG CHILDREN'S BEHAVIOR:
Implementing Your Goals
A variety of up-to-date approaches to discipline and guidance to help you deal more effectively with children. Also an excellent addition to CDA and competency-based training programs.

HL-015-4 $ 8.95

FINGERPLAYS & RHYMES
Delight children 2-8 while teaching them about numbers, colors, shapes, holidays, self-concept, feelings, and much more. More than 250 original rhymes and fingerplays.

HL-083-9 $14.95

STORYBOOK CLASSROOMS:
Using Children's Literature in the Learning Center/Primary Grades
A guide to making effective use of children's literature in the classroom. Activities designed for independent use by children K-3, supplemented with illustrations and patterns for easy use. Guidelines, suggestions, and bibliographies will delight and help to instill a love of reading in kids!

HL-043-X $16.95

ACTIVITY BOOKS

EARLY CHILDHOOD ACTIVITIES:
A Treasury of Ideas from Worldwide Sources
A virtual encyclopedia of projects, games and activities for children aged 3-7, containing over 500 different child-tested activities drawn from a variety of teaching systems. The ultimate activity book!

HL-066-9 $16.95

VANILLA MANILA FOLDER GAMES
Make exciting and stimulating **Vanilla Manila Folder Games** quickly and easily with simple manila file folders and colored marking pens. Unique learning activities designed for children aged 3-8.

HL-059-6 $16.95

LEAVES ARE FALLING IN RAINBOWS
Science Activities for Early Childhood
Hundreds of science activities help your children learn concepts and properties of water, air, plants, light, shadows, magnets, sound and electricity. Build on interests when providing science experience and they'll **always** be eager to learn!

HL-045-6 $16.95

HANDBOOK OF LEARNING ACTIVITIES
Over 125 exciting, enjoyable activities and projects for young children in the areas of math, health and safety, play, movement, science, social studies, art, language development, puppetry and more!

HL-058-8 $16.95

MONTH BY MONTH ACTIVITY GUIDE FOR THE PRIMARY GRADES
Month by Month gives you a succinct guide to the effective recruitment and utilization of teachers' aides plus a **full year's worth** of fun-filled education activities in such areas as reading, math, art, and science.

HL-061-8 $16.95

ART PROJECTS FOR YOUNG CHILDREN
Build a basic art program of stimulating projects on a limited budget and time schedule with **Art Projects**. Contains over 100 fun-filled projects in the areas of drawing, painting, puppets, clay, printing and more!

HL-051-0 $16.95

BLOOMIN' BULLETIN BOARDS
Stimulate active student participation and learning as you promote your kids' creativity with these delightful and entertaining activities in the areas of Art, Language Arts, Mathematics, Health, Science, Social Studies, and the Holidays. Watch learning skills and self-concepts blossom!

HL-047-2 $14.95

AEROSPACE PROJECTS FOR YOUNG CHILDREN
Introduce children to the fascinating field of aerospace with the exciting and informative projects and field trip suggestions. Contributors include over 30 aviation/aerospace agencies and personnel.

HL-052-9 $14.95

CHILD'S PLAY:
An Activities and Materials Handbook
An eclectic selection of fun-filled activities for preschool children designed to lend excitement to the learning process. Activities include puppets, mobiles, poetry, songs and more.

HL-003-0 $14.95

ENERGY:
A Curriculum for 3, 4 and 5 Year Olds
Help preschool children become aware of what energy is, the sources of energy, the uses of energy and wise energy use with the fun-filled activities, songs and games included in this innovative manual.

HL-069-3 $ 9.95

HUMANICS LEARNING

Send Orders To:

Humanics Learning
P.O. Box 7447
Atlanta, Ga. 30309

ORDER FORM

Name _____

Address _____

City _____ State _____ Zip _____

TITLE	CODE	PRICE	QUANTITY	TOTAL

All orders from individuals must include prepayment, or credit card number and signature must be provided below.

☐ MasterCard   ☐ Visa

_____
Account Number

_____
Signature

_____
MasterCard Interbank No.   Expiration Date

_____
Institutional Purchase Order

SUBTOTAL	
Ga. Residents, add 5% sales tax	
Discount, if applicable	
Shipping and Handling	
TOTAL	

Shipping and Handling Charges

Up to $10.00 add	$2.00
$10.01 to $20.00 add	$3.00
$20.01 to $40.00 add	$4.00
$40.01 to $70.00 add	$5.00
$70.01 to $100.00 add	$6.00
$100.01 to $125.00 add	$7.00
$125.01 to $150.00 add	$8.00
$150.01 to $175.00 add	$9.00
$175.01 to $200.00 add	$10.00

Orders over $200 vary depending on method of shipment.

☎ ORDER TOLL FREE
1-800-874-8844

• **Same Day Telephone Service —**
Order toll free and we will ship your order within 48 hours.

• **Order By Phone —**
with Visa or MasterCard

Please call for discounts and terms.